how to get what YOU want

WALKER BOOKS

AND SUBSIDIARIES

LONDON · BOSTON · SYDNEY · AUCKLAND

HOW TO GET WHAT YOU WANT

has been written for anyone at a crossroads in their life. Maybe you've just left university or school or are deciding whether or not to do so. Maybe you've stopped studying altogether and are wondering what to do next. This book will help you choose.

All about you

How to Get What You Want is very much about you. It's about discovering your wildest dreams and fantasies and your biggest fears and anxieties then seeing how you can get through those fears and anxieties to make your dreams come true.

Exploring your mind

Much of what's in this book you probably won't have thought about before, but, if you have, then that's great because the concepts will be familiar. There are lots of new ideas to explore and, once you've tapped into them, you'll be able to expand on them for the rest of your life.

Why these chapters?

Each chapter is based on the "Puzzle of Life", a puzzle I created from listening to the people I worked with in Life Clubs, and hearing what was important to them. It takes you through the various key themes your life falls into. By working on the different puzzle pieces (or, in this case, chapters), you'll gain the knowledge and confidence to be what you want to be.

How to use this book

Dip into this book as often as you like and for as long as you like – whether that's five minutes or five hours. It's not a novel that you read from cover to cover – though you can if you want to. Within each chapter of How to Get What You Want are questions that will be relevant to you. These questions are inspired by my observations of the young people I've worked with who are actively thinking about what's important to them in their lives.

Find a question that's relevant

Look through the list on pages 6-7 and see if any jump out at you. Once you find one that does, get curious. Read the answer and think about what actions you could take related to that question. Move to the next question, keep exploring. Find or buy a blank "Me" notebook to keep alongside you, or use scrap pieces of paper and slip them inside the cover so you don't lose them. This book is about you, so do whatever feels the most comfortable for you.

Or do something completely different

Why not open the book at a random page and see what happens. Just go with the flow.

PUZZLE OF LIFE

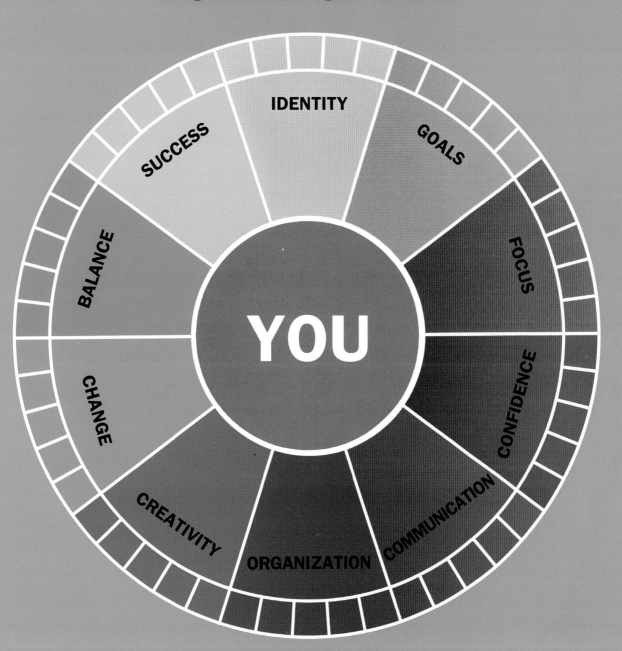

Identity

At the top of the puzzle is "Identity" because knowing who you are is really the first step to discovering what you want your life to be like – what you want out of life.

Goals

From there you move onto "Goals", because once you've discovered what's important to you, you can begin setting goals. No matter how big or small your goal is, just having one goal gives you a feeling of moving forward and knowing what you want to achieve.

Focus

Once you've decided on how you want to move forward, it's essential to "Focus". So many of us go off on tangents and fritter our energy away. When you focus you can ensure you move towards your goal.

Confidence

"Confidence" is something everyone lacks in some area of their life and, even those of you who feel confident in particular areas, confess to wanting more. Once you're feeling confident even focusing on the most difficult goal becomes easier.

Communication

When you've worked out what you want to focus on and are feeling confident and ready to go, you can start on "Communication". It's great to tell people so they can understand what's going on and can give you a real sense of support.

Organization

So many of us find it hard to manage our time and daily routine. "Organization" is of key importance in order to achieve anything.

Creativity

And, to balance organization, or enhance it, "Creativity" is both fun and vital. Imagination is an essential part of change and creativity is about doing things differently.

Change

Life is all about "Change" – changing anything and everything you want. Making your life your own. Whether you've created change or it's been thrust upon you, change is something to understand and that's why it's another important theme.

Balance

If you're facing change, the first place to look is at the "Balance" in your life. Balance is the key to living a harmonious life. Once you're aware of all the different forces in your life and the ways you can balance them, you'll find you feel happier.

Success

And, finally, "Success" – what we all want. For each of us it will be something different. By the end of this book, you'll have discovered what success means to you.

After reading this book I'd like you to feel **comfortable**, **enthusiastic**, **relaxed** and …

HAPPY TO BE YOU.

Nina Grunfeld

CONTENTS

IDENTITY

> **"Unlike a drop of water which loses its identity when it joins the ocean, man does not lose his being in the society in which he lives. Man's life is independent."**
> B. R. Ambedkar

Who am I?
What makes me special?
What makes me ME?

Ever asked yourself questions like these? If you don't know who you are, it can make you feel under-confident and worried that you are presenting yourself "wrongly". You may feel you want other people to tell you what they like about you but, although that is always interesting to hear, it's not who you really are – it's who they think you are.

So, rather than worry about what others think of you, let's start celebrating that you are special and totally unique. This section is all about your identity – how you feel about yourself, who you think you are and what is important to you.

1. WHAT MAKES ME ME?

One of the fundamental parts of you is your values ... your principles. They're one of the things that make you unique.

What are values?

Here are a few values: generosity, freedom, kindness, equality, trust, humour, being connected, adventure, respect, honesty, fairness, thoughtfulness. If any make you think "Yes!" as you read them, then they're yours.

Why are values important?

Imagine you want to join a hockey team or choir, but when you start you don't enjoy it. This could be because having to practise every evening is restricting your freedom and freedom is a key value for you. So, you had a dream, but it wasn't the right dream. Once you know your values you can start dreaming of things that are **really** you.

How to find your values

Ask yourself a question, such as "What would be my perfect day?" or "What would I do if I were Prime Minister?" or "What do I like about my friends?" Write down your answers and question them! Ask yourself "What's important to me about that?" for each answer.

You can ask this question about anything at any time. If you are feeling particularly happy, check why you're feeling so happy.

ONCE YOU FIND YOUR VALUES YOU CAN USE THEM FOR MAKING DECISIONS.

Remember your values

Keep a list of your values as they will help you make decisions about your future and allow you to understand yourself better. For example, if "privacy" is an important value, you may want some time on your own during the day. If "generosity" is one of your values you may enjoy tutoring a friend or helping your mum with the cooking.

What are your values?

Ask yourself what you like about your friends. If they make you laugh, "laughter" or "humour" might be two of your values. What else do you like about them? If you think they're kind, "kindness" might be a value for you.

Keep questioning each of your answers. Ask yourself what's important to you about "humour" or "kindness". If your answer is that they think of you, "thoughtfulness" might be a value. If your answer is that they respect you "respect" might be a value.

FINDING YOUR VALUES WILL HELP YOU KNOW WHO YOU ARE

2. WHAT DO I WANT TO DO WITH MY LIFE?

Somewhere deep down you already have the answer to this question, so enjoy finding out. One way of doing this is by creating a collage.

Take a whole lot of magazines and pull out all the pictures that really mean something to you, pictures that feel exciting and personal. Don't just pull them out because on the surface they appeal, make sure they are really important to you. For example, don't just choose a picture of a celebrity looking good, but choose a picture of somewhere you'd like to live or a t-shirt that you really like. Once you've cut out loads of pictures, stick them onto a huge bit of paper. These images are a key to what you want to do with your life.

Ask yourself three questions

1. *What's important to me about each one of these pictures?*

2. *What is the one picture that instantly jumps out at me?*

3. *What do I like so much about that one picture?*

SARAH'S STORY

Sarah's room was one gigantic collage. Two walls were filled with photos she had taken of all her friends, on another wall were pictures from fashion magazines and quotes about life, and the fourth wall was covered in train tickets she and her friends had used. Apart from her obvious interest in photography, Sarah's room told lots of stories of people and adventures. In the holidays, Sarah enrolled on a part-time photojournalism course while doing work experience on her local paper.

TIM'S STORY

Tim's collage was full of advertising slogans and pictures. Bits of comic books and music posters were stuck next to maps and pictures of influential figures from Chairman Mao to Che Guevara. Tim saw that he was interested in the way the world worked and decided he'd like to study politics at university.

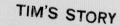

JUST DO IT

USE PICTURES TO HELP YOU DISCOVER WHAT YOU WANT

3. WHAT AM I GOOD AT?

If you don't feel you shine at something that exists already, create something new to be a star in.

It's easy to feel that you're not good at anything, but just because you don't like any of the subjects on the curriculum or the job you do doesn't mean you're a failure. It just means that your interests lie elsewhere.

What are your talents?

Everything that you love doing, you love doing because …
• you are already good at it
• you are good at one bit of it
• you can see that you could get good at it

Let's call all of those things your talents and discover them.

There's a 5-step process to doing this. Take your time – there's no need to do everything at once. Just keep thinking about them and add to each list as the days go by.

STEP 1

When you were young
Think back to all the things you loved as a small child and write them down. It may help to brainstorm them with a friend or with someone who remembers you as a small child – and to look at some old photos, too.

Here are some ideas to get you started:
cycling
making sandcastles
dressing up
football
playing with dolls or cars
fishing
reading
playing shop
painting
singing
riding
listening to mum chatting on the phone
making models

What can you think of?

STEP 2

Now
Write down all the things you love doing now. Again, make a list of them.

For example:
photography
camping
gossiping
tennis
cooking
swimming
music
surfing the net
dancing
shopping
gardening
reading
cycling
making films
texting
going to gigs

What can you think of?

STEP 3

Fantasy

You're now going to go (a little) wild. Don't worry about whether or not you've got enough money or education, this is fantasy time. What would you do if you could do absolutely anything you liked? You may have looked at someone or read about someone and thought "I'd like their life." Write down what it was about their life that you liked. Write down as many fantasies as you want – each one will reveal something about you.

For example:

fly to the moon
become an actor
build my own home
sail round the world
make a CD
invent a cure for cancer
go to the North Pole
write a bestselling novel
play sport for my country
design a bicycle
run a business
teach abroad
make a film
start a blog

What can you think of?

STEP 4

What you want to learn

The final list you're going to write is of everything you'd like to learn and, again, money is no object.

For example:

kung fu
beauty tips
driving
guitar
design
a new language
scuba diving
golf
painting
salsa
flying
dressmaking
archaeology

Make the list as long as you want.

> JUST GO FOR IT.

ALLOW YOUR PAST TO POINT TO YOUR FUTURE

STEP 5

Find out your values

Now go through everything in your four lists and find out what's really important to you about each thing you've written down.

Once you've discovered your values you can see how you can use your talents in the present and future.

For example:

What I really liked about singing was …
• being part of a group
• making a beautiful noise
• feeling special
• being on the stage

What I really like about the idea of sailing round the world is …
• freedom
• exploration
• seeing the world
• learning about fish

Understand what's really important to you about everything on your lists. There's no rush. Dip in and out of each list when you want to. By now you will have discovered not only what you're good at, but also how you can use these talents in the future.

4. HOW DO I FIND

A love of cooking meant something totally different to John and Chrissie. It pointed out different values and talents for them both.

JOHN'S STORY

COOKING

John likes cooking because he likes caring for others.

VALUES

Two of John's values are: caring, looking after others.

TALENTS

John will find happiness by using his "caring" talents to work with other people, whether it's in a hotel, a hospital, in recruitment, training, etc.

MY TALENTS?

CHRISSIE'S STORY

COOKING
Chrissie likes cooking because it's creative – you make something completely new.

VALUES
Two of Chrissie's values are: creativity, making something out of nothing.

TALENTS
Chrissie will find happiness using her creative talents – whether it's baking a cake or starting her own business.

USE VALUES TO DISCOVER YOUR FUTURE

5. WHAT AM I REALLY LIKE?

It can feel a bit destabilizing not being sure what's special about yourself. There is a way of finding out exactly what you're like which is simple, fun and worth thinking about.

Judging others

Make a list of people you know (or famous people) and write down how you'd describe them. Not visual stuff – attractive, sexy, handsome, etc., but what they are like as people – honest, untogether, brave, etc. Be as specific as you can.

Are you like them?

Look at your list. It may sound weird but we do talk about other people using adjectives that we would use to describe ourselves, so the adjectives you have used for people on your list are also adjectives that could describe you. If, for example, you've written down that someone is flamboyant, just think about how you might be flamboyant and, conversely, if you say someone is indecisive, just think about how you might be indecisive, too.

Explore your words

Explore what you mean by each word. If you describe someone as energetic, are they vibrant, speedy, vital, active, dynamic, etc? Whichever it is, that's the one that you are too. If you find it difficult, go back to your values and make sure you know what's important to you about every word.

Once you've tried and tested this theory, keep an ear open as to how you're describing others. It's a fun game. You can be thinking, "Oh, that person's intelligent" and then realize that you are, too.

FIND OUT WHAT YOU'RE REALLY LIKE FROM THE WAY YOU JUDGE OTHERS.

THE WAY YOU DESCRIBE PEOPLE DESCRIBES YOU, TOO

6. WHY DO I THINK WHAT

Who knows why you think what you think? But you can try and find out.

Most thoughts come from a combination of family, friends, teachers, other adults and, of course, yourself. And you can often trace where they came from using a kind of family tree.

I THINK?

Why do you want to trace your thoughts?

Most of us have lots of unhelpful ideas about ourselves, such as "I'm no good at science" or "I'm hopeless at relationships". Find out which person in your family these negative thoughts have come from. Then find evidence in your family tree to support totally different, positive thoughts.

It doesn't matter if you're adopted or don't know much about your family. You can still build up a picture.

Step 1: Draw your family tree

This family tree is not like those family trees that stretch back hundreds of years. Simply draw three generations of your family tree – you and your generation (include sisters, brothers, cousins, step- and half-brothers and sisters), then your parents and uncles and aunts (include all partners) and then your grandparents and their brothers and sisters and partners. Put in everyone you can think of. They don't have to be blood relations.

Step 2: Follow the ideas

As you draw your family tree, remember all the beliefs you have about yourself ("I'm not creative", "None of my family are good at sport", "We're all fat" etc.) – and discover where those beliefs came from. For example, from whom did you first hear, "None of my family is good at making money"? How did you jump to that conclusion? Then, find the opposite of this in your family tree. Find at least one person who is excellent at making money. Challenge all your assumptions as, once you do, you have a choice as to what you want to think.

TRY IT – IT WORKS

YOU DON'T HAVE TO BELIEVE YOUR NEGATIVE THOUGHTS

7. WHAT CAN I DO TO FIT IN?

It would be great if you could do nothing and wait for everyone else to fit in with you, but sadly we don't always have the confidence to do that.

Most of us want to be liked and accepted as part of a group, rather than start one of our own. When you feel like you don't fit in, you can feel awkward, as if everything you do is wrong. Your jokes don't feel funny, your clothes don't seem right and your body feels clumsy. And yet it's you who is judging yourself – quite probably no one else is thinking the same thing.

Find a different perspective

Imagine that there is no "wrong", that nothing you say could ever be "wrong" (unless it was hurtful). In class you would never be "wrong", in your job you would never be "wrong", with your family you would never be "wrong".

Now imagine that there's no "right" either. That your friends aren't "right" when they say things or make jokes. What they say is as "wrong" or as "right" as what you say. How does that make you feel?

You're fine as you are

Once you change your perspective to a no one is "right" and no one is "wrong" perspective (or even a we are all "right" perspective) you'll stop being so hard on yourself and realize that it's not that difficult to fit in. You're fine as you are – "right" or "wrong".

DON'T TRY AND FIT IN, BE YOURSELF — YOU'RE "RIGHT" AS YOU ARE

8. WHY AM I HERE?

Have you ever found yourself asking, "Why am I here?" or "What is my purpose on this planet?"

IDENTITY

Have you ever asked yourself questions like these?

Most of us have. And, who really knows, maybe there isn't a reason for being here. But it's really inspiring and exciting to have a vision of your future – whether it's a plan for the day (small vision) or for the rest of your life (big vision).

You'll naturally be either a big or a small vision person, but for now have a go at both.

Find your small vision

On a blank piece of paper, use the headings below to inspire you to write a short CV, dated one year from now. This CV is just for you (not for a potential employer) and, when it's finished, you'll know why you're here and what to aim for, at least for the next twelve months.

My address:

My qualifications:

I'm studying/My job is:

Experiences I've gained:

My role in my family is:

I'm the kind of friend who:

The work I do in the community is:

Find your big vision

Take another sheet of blank paper and on it, using the ideas below, write the speech someone else is giving about you at your birthday party five (or even ten) years from now. Think about what you'll have achieved as much as what type of person you are. Once you've completed this speech, you'll know why you are here. You'll have worked out your purpose for the next few years. Here are some ideas to start you off:

- Congratulations to [insert your name here] on your birthday.
- Where you live now.
- What they say about you in your local community.
- What you studied.
- What your job is.
- What family you have now (or plan to have).
- What your family has been saying about you.
- Who your friends are and what they have been saying about you.

USE FUTURE PERSPECTIVES TO WORK OUT WHAT YOU WANT TO DO NEXT

"Without having a goal, it's difficult to score."

Paul Arden

What does the word "goal" mean to you?

It may sound more like a football term than anything useful, but this football word is more relevant to your life than you think. In this section you're going to discover what your goals are and how to achieve them. And you're going to set some. Each goal gives you a direction and achieving your goal will make you feel as good as you would if you'd scored at football – or maybe even better.

1. HOW DO I FIND GOALS?

Up until now you may have been given most of your goals by other people. For example, "You've got exams, get on with your revision" or "What work experience have you got?" Now is the time to choose your own goals.

There are two ways to find your goals
Either look back at your big and small visions (p25) and see if there is an idea there that you feel inspired to turn into a goal, or make a Balance Chart (p30). The Balance Chart breaks down your life into different areas so you can understand what's going on, which will help you set goals. Have a go.

What are your goals?

Without calling them goals, you might have wanted a cooler-looking bedroom, to get fit, or to catch up on your sleep. Or maybe you haven't really thought in terms of the future and having goals at all and don't know where to begin. Your life might feel like a blur with nothing in the long-term view at all; no particular path emerging.

♣ Rest & Relaxation

When you wake up do you bounce out of bed or are you tired all the time? Do you go to bed really late? Do you sleep in really late? What relaxes you? Do you feel you spend your life studying, working or partying, with no time to relax? Do you feel stressed? Do you get headaches? Stomach aches? Skin problems?

♠ Home

Do you like where you live? Does the thought of going home make you happy? Do you have your own bedroom? Do you like your room? Is there somewhere for you to work and play as well as sleep? Do you get on with everyone you live with?

♦ Creativity

Classic creativity is about painting, playing an instrument, designing, writing, etc. Do you enjoy any of these activities or something similar – blogging, DJ-ing, etc.? Creativity can work in other areas, too. It can be about having good conversations, pushing yourself to do things differently from the way you usually do them or being open to new people and ideas. How creative are you feeling? Do you have time to be creative?

♥ Health & Fitness

How healthy are you? How much do you use your body? Do you enjoy sport? Do you pay attention to your body? What sort of food do you put in it? How much alcohol? How many cigarettes? Are you looking after your body or neglecting and abusing it?

Make your Balance Chart

Allow for ten areas and, taking each one in turn, score each area of your life with a number between one and ten. Ten means you feel totally satisfied in that area, one means that that area isn't great for you right now. This isn't a test – you're not aiming to get all tens, you're aiming to find out what's important to you and what you'd like to change. Once you know where you'd like your life to be different you can start setting goals.

About your life

To get started, read the descriptions below and give each of them a number that feels right for you in that area now. Each time you fill in your Balance Chart the score will change depending on what is going on in your life.

♠ Friends & Social Life

Are your friends always there for you when you want them? Do you have a few really good mates? Is there someone you can confide in? Do you know what you like doing when you go out – and do you get to do it? Do you do what your friends suggest or do they do what you suggest? Do you enjoy being with your friends or do they bore you?

♥ Family

How well do you get on with your family? Are there other families you'd rather have than yours? What do you value about them that's missing from your family? Are your family always nagging you or are they supportive? Do you ever spend time with them? Do you enjoy it when you do? Do you feel your family are allowing you to grow up and change?

♦ Money

Do you have enough money? When you get money is it in your pocket one minute and spent the next? Do you like spending money? Are you good at planning? Do you find it easy to save? Is there anything that you're saving up for?

♣ Work & College

Whether you're at school or college or have a job, are you happy with what you're doing? Would you like to get some more qualifications or different ones? Do you work hard? Do you feel you know what you want to do with your life? Do you enjoy what you do or do you live for the weekends?

♠ Spirituality

Are you religious, do you dislike the thought of religion or are you somewhere in-between? Do you know what's important to you – what your values are, what your purpose is? Do you meditate? Do you feel you need spirituality? Is spirituality of any interest to you? (If not, and you don't care, score yourself high.)

♥ Love & Relationships

Are you happy with your love life? Do you have a boyfriend/girlfriend? Do you want one? Are you good at looking after yourself? Do you laugh a lot? Do you look after yourself as well as you would your best friend? Circle two numbers in this area – one for the way you feel about someone else and one for the the way you feel about yourself.

The Balance Chart

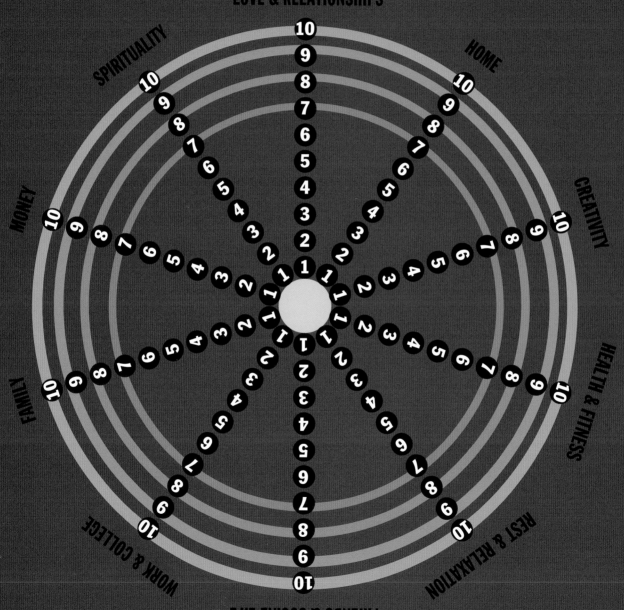

Choose your goal

Look at the scores you've marked on the Balance Chart. You can now set a goal either in an area that you scored low in to bring it up or in an area that you scored high in to amplify it.

Let's say that you're scoring high in Love & Relationships. You've just met someone and you're feeling really happy. You're spending every moment of every day together and loving it. But because you haven't got that much money between you, you're hanging out at fast food venues or pubs and your Health & Fitness is suffering.

Either: Set a large or a small goal to improve your Health & Fitness score (area you're low in).

- Small goal – Next time we go out, I'm going to make a healthy picnic to take with us and we can eat outside.

- Large goal – I'm going to run three times a week in the morning.

Or: Set a large or small goal to improve your Love & Relationships score (area you're high in).

- Small goal – I'm going to write him/her a letter showing how much I appreciate them.

- Large goal – I'm going to organize something really special for them.

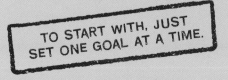

TO START WITH, JUST SET ONE GOAL AT A TIME.

USE THE BALANCE CHART TO UNDERSTAND YOURSELF AND YOUR LIFE

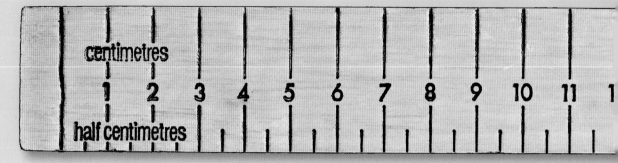

Yes. There are rules. Not that many and all very sensible. Here are five worth remembering.

1. Make the goal about yourself and something you can do by yourself.

You can't change anyone else, so there's no point in making a goal that involves anyone else.

For example, "I want to go out with Charlie". You may well want that date, but ultimately it's Charlie's choice as well, so it can't be a goal.

What can be a goal? "I want to be available/ready/prepared to go out with Charlie" or "I want to ask Charlie out" could both be goals, but don't feel despondent if Charlie says no.

It is much better to set goals about yourself such as, "I want to feel good about being alone, so that when I do meet someone I like, we can have a great relationship".

2. Make your goal positive.

Has anyone ever told you not to think about something and then that's all you can think of? Try it now. Well, it's the same with goals.

For example, "I won't eat chocolate" will get you thinking about chocolate until you have to eat it. A positive goal might be, "I will eat healthily" or "I will enjoy snacking on celery/carrots". Similarly "I won't bite my nails" or "I won't waste time" are both negative goals that can be replaced with, "I have lovely long nails" and "I enjoy getting things done".

3. Imagine you've already achieved your goal.

Try writing your goal in the present tense as if you've already achieved it. If you think, "I'm going to be an actor" (future tense) that sounds good, but not very motivational. If you start thinking "I am an actor", in your mind you've already got to where you want to be.

GOAL-SETTING?

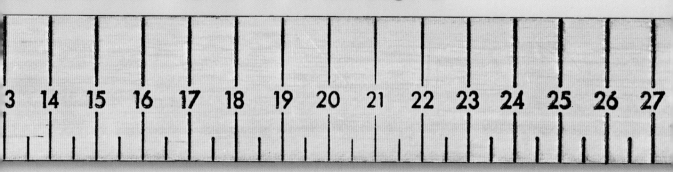

This can be very inspirational and very helpful. You can then ask yourself: "If I'm an actor, what would I do next?"

Set goals like "I weigh 60 kilos" or "I am top at maths" or "I have a great conversation with my mum every week". The idea of already having achieved your goal will make it easier to achieve.

4. Make your goal measurable.

Give your goal a time when you're going to start it and a time by when you want to have achieved it and make it something you can measure.

If you want to do things differently it's important to be specific about what you want to do. For example, "From tonight I want to spend two hours revising every night until after exams" or "From today I want to talk to one new person every evening" are measurable, whereas "I want to stop spending so long on the Internet" or "I want to go out more" aren't.

Make sure your goals are realistic. Give yourself more time in which to achieve them, rather than less.

5. Be sure you really want to achieve your goal.

You know what it's like when you say you'll do something, but you don't really want to. It can become a real pain. It's the same with setting a goal. Make sure it's a goal you feel really committed to, otherwise you're setting yourself up with a goal you don't really want to achieve and probably won't.

You might say, "I ought to talk to Mr Jones about my project". There's no energy behind that goal at all. If you can make it, "I want to talk to Mr Jones", there's a chance you'll succeed.

Listen to your language when you think about the goal you're setting. Words like *should, ought, need* and *must* don't belong in goals.

> **When it is obvious that the goals cannot be reached, don't adjust the goals, adjust the action steps.**
> Confucius

For example, take the goal of making lots of money for travelling and see how that breaks down into masses of little stones.

Some goals are really big and you can feel so overwhelmed that you just give up. Don't.

If your goals are too big, break them down into small enough activities that they become achievable. Imagine your goal as an enormous rock. You are going to smash it up into rubble which you can then tackle one stone at a time.

Break your goals down

A way of breaking goals down is to use a spider diagram. You can see how it works here and then create your own. Your big goal is in the centre, each "arm" is a plan and each "hair" on each "arm" is an easily achievable stone ready to go. Have a go at breaking down your goals this way.

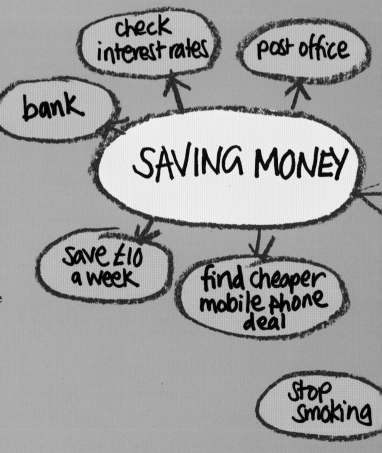

GOAL LESS SCARY?

newsagents ad

baby sitting

flyer drop

get references

write CV

buy newspaper

EVENING AND WEEKEND WORK

read ads

ask everyone I know

teach Spanish

work in pub

HOLIDAY JOB

MONEY-MAKING SCHEME

ECONOMIZING

no new clothes

don't eat out

stop going to pub

BREAK YOUR GOALS DOWN

4. IS THERE A FUN WAY TO SET GOALS?

If you still feel daunted by the idea of setting goals, have fun with this way of doing it.

Write your own headline

You know those headlines in newspapers that make you want to read the rest of the article? You're going to write one about yourself. If you want to be top of maths, your headline might read **Jenny top of maths class and not just by a fraction** or, if you want to get fit, your headline could say **New look John uses his washboard abs to clean clothes.** Try some for yourself.

Prepare to change your mind

Be open as to what your goal is really about. When you start writing your headline you may realize that the goal you thought you wanted isn't what you really want.

For example, if your headline is, "I want to lose weight to look good" you may have thought you want to get thin to look good. Now you might realize that you want to get thinner because you imagine that being thinner (and healthier) will help you play better tennis. Your new headline could be, **Slim Jessica wins tennis match** and you can then adjust your goal.

Expert tips

- Make your headline short – under fifteen words long.
- Use action verbs, such as *power, steam* and *build.*
- Make verbs even more active by ending them in "ing" such as *launching, running* and *opening.*
- Experiment with visual expressions, for example, *flat out, sharp* and *expands.*

> START WITH THE MOST IMPORTANT THING – YOU.

THE
DAILY GOAL

SLIM JESSICA WINS TENNIS MATCH

5. HOW DO I WORK OUT WHA

When you've got a plan, you're in charge and you'll get something that you wanted done which feels good. But it can be difficult to know what your plan is.

It can be quite frustrating when you don't have a plan. For example, someone phones up and asks you to hang out with them. You go along and then someone else asks you over to their place and then maybe someone else suggests the cinema or a meal and at the end of the day, maybe it's been fun, but you feel as if you haven't really made good use of that day.

How to make a plan

There's an incredibly powerful, but simple way to find out what you want for the future and all it involves is drawing circles – two big ones and lots of little ones.

1. Draw a big circle – about 20 centimetres in diameter. That circle is your life as it is now.

2. Draw yourself as a circle – any size and anywhere – within that circle (put your initials in that circle).

3. Now draw more circles. Draw one circle for everyone important in your life and one circle for everything important to you (education, interests, sport, illnesses, religion, activities, work, arguments, etc.). Depending on where they fit into your life, place them inside or outside your big circle. Be as spontaneous as possible, not everything has to be positive.

Each circle can be as big or small as you want (depending on its importance to you) and as close or as far away from you as you want. These circles can overlap and they can be outside the large circle (your life) as well. Be totally honest about where you want to put each circle and what size you want it to be. Label each circle so you remember what they each stand for.

4. Ask yourself some questions about your circle, such as :
- Do you like the picture you've created?
- Has anything you hadn't thought about before come up?
- Why are some of the circles bigger/smaller than others?
- Why are some of the circles closer/further away from you than others?
- Why are some overlapping/outside the circle and others aren't?
- How do some of the circles (be specific) affect the others?
- If you could shrink/expand a circle (be specific), what might happen?

5. Draw another big circle – about 20 centimetres in diameter – that circle is your life in two years' time.

WANT?

6. Again, draw yourself as a circle any size and anywhere within that circle. Imagine who you'd like to be and how you'd like to feel in two years.

7. Now place other circles in (or outside) the main circle. Draw one circle for everyone who you'd like to be important in your life and one circle for everything that you'd like to be important to you two years from now. Again, be as spontaneous as possible.

8. Ask yourself some questions about your circle, such as:
• What's significantly changed?
• What caused those changes to happen?

JUST GET CURIOUS ABOUT EVERYTHING YOU'VE DRAWN.

OLLIE'S STORY

Although Ollie really liked his new girlfriend, Chrissie, they both hung around with Jen, Ollie's best female friend who he secretly fancied. Chrissie complained sometimes but Ollie always dismissed her moans and said "You're just jealous". However when Ollie drew his first circle, representing his life today, he could clearly see that although he put Chrissie's circle right next to him, he put Jen's next to him too, only on the other side. Ollie understood that Chrissie was right and that he was being pulled in two places trying to please both Chrissie and Jen at the same time.

The next circle Ollie drew, depicting his life in two years time, had Jen smaller and at the edge of his life and Chrissie large and overlapping him. Ollie knew what he had to do next. He began to see less of Jen and more of Chrissie.

YOUR SUBCONSCIOUS USUALLY KNOWS WHAT YOU WANT

6. HOW CAN I STICK TO MY GOAL?

If you've failed at sticking to your New Year's resolution in the past, don't worry. New Year's resolutions aren't typical of the goals we set, which is why most people don't stick to them.

Did your resolution tick all the five rules of goal-setting (p32) or was it something you felt you ought to do? If you think about all the activities you still love from early childhood and the friends you've had for many years, you can see how loyal you can be to the things you've started.

Keep your natural motivation

Babies don't lie on their backs forever and gurgle, they get up and walk and talk. As you get older, you'll want to keep moving forwards, and yet sometimes you might pick the wrong goal or you'll be put off by family or friends saying, "That doesn't sound like you" or "That's going to be tricky". Then you get to a stage where you say these things to yourself.

What keeps you going?

Often the reason you don't keep going with what you've started is that you forget what has motivated you. Let's take that friendship you've had since you were eleven. Why have you stayed friends? Laughter? Competitiveness? Trust? What about those activities you've done since you were quite small. What's kept you going with them?

Find your motivational tools

Once you start becoming aware of the reasons you've kept doing something, you can bring those motivational tools into everything you do. There's no longer any reason why you shouldn't achieve what you want to achieve. Start collecting your toolkit. You can use these tools when you're about to start a project or whenever you feel you might give up. Once you know how to set your goals and keep yourself motivated there'll be no stopping you.

Which of these motivational tools works for you?

Rewards: a cup of tea, money, phone call with a friend
Inspiration: feeling inspired to succeed
Proving your worth: to parents, teachers, friends
Competition: against yourself, or someone else
Team spirit: getting support, enthusiasm and encouragement

DAVID'S STORY

David wanted to lose weight but kept giving up. He thought he was useless at sticking to his goals until he remembered all the things he'd stuck to in the past. David had loved cooking since he'd helped his mum bake cakes aged six. Cooking was creative, he enjoyed the taste of what he made and it made him feel useful around the house. David also remembered that he'd been best friends with his neighbour since before he started school – they had fun together and laughed a lot. Thinking about it, David realized he had a set of motivational tools that could help him lose weight (creativity, being in control of tastes, feeling useful, enjoyment and fun). Together with his mum, David used his creativity to come up with different healthy meals, which he made sure he liked the taste of and, in order to feel useful, David said to his mum that he'd shop for the food every day on the way home. Next David found an exercise that he could enjoy – dancing – and he started playing squash too which he found fun. The weight dropped off.

COLLECT YOUR MOTIVATIONAL TOOLKIT NOW

"Take up one idea. Make that one idea your life – think of it, dream of it, live on that idea. Let the brain, muscles, nerves, every part of your body, be full of that idea, and just leave every other idea alone. This is the way to success."

Swami Vivekananda

1. WHICH GOAL SHOULD I FOCUS ON?

OK, so you've set your goals, but which one do you want to start with?

Maybe you've set too many goals. Maybe all your goals feel as if they're intertwined. If you feel as if all your options are pulling you in different directions, start focusing. Focusing is all about getting started. It usually doesn't matter where you start. If you focus on one goal at a time, like using a magnifying glass to light a fire, all your energy will be centred on one thing for maximum impact.

How do you make decisions?

You can spend ages debating about what to do next. Sometimes you might ask different people and get lots of different answers. At other times you might write lists with pros and cons or toss a coin. Often none of these methods do any good and you remain as confused as you were. Indecision wastes time and can sap your energy and your spirit. It can make you feel a failure.

All roads lead to Rome

In order to move forward you sometimes have to decide on one course of action and make it your goal. It really doesn't matter which goal you choose, so long as you focus on just one.

Finding your intuition

A great way to access your intuition is to ask yourself "Which goal would make the biggest difference to my life if I focused on it right now?" You'll usually find you know the answer.

Refocusing

Focusing is also about learning how to refocus when you've been interrupted. Once the interruption has gone away you can use your mind to refocus and move forward.

Use the Balance Chart

The Balance Chart (p30) is another good place to work out what you want. Look at your Balance Chart and work out which area of your life you'd like to focus on right now. And then go for it.

ALEX'S STORY

Alex wanted to travel after school ended, but she didn't know where to go or who to go with or what to do when she got there. She wanted to organize her gap year, but she had too many options.

Alex's list of options went like this:
• Go to Berlin with Jo and study German.
• Travel round India with Sam and work in a school.
• Stay at home doing temp work and learning to scuba dive and then travel with Flo teaching scuba diving.

Looking at her Balance Chart, Alex could see her money score was low. Suddenly her first goal became very straight forward – to look for a job and earn some money. Alex had focused. She decided it would be cheapest to stay at home and get a job and, at the same time, learn to scuba dive. If this worked out, she could travel with Flo, meet up with Sam in India and, maybe, if she had enough money and the dates worked out, study German with Jo in Berlin later in the year. Alex had a plan.

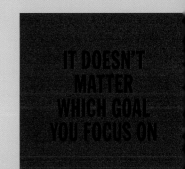

IT DOESN'T MATTER WHICH GOAL YOU FOCUS ON

2. HOW CAN I NARROW THINGS DOWN?

You may have lots of ideas and want to do all of them.
You still want to focus.

If you try to divide your time between projects you may feel you're spreading yourself a bit thin and not doing any of them really well. Or you may feel that there are too many ideas whizzing around your head and you're not able to concentrate on anything.

Keep a book of thoughts

A great idea if you are really creative is to write down everything you think of that you want to do. Get a folder and write up each idea as fully as you can. Use drawings and spider diagrams so you make sure you won't forget them.

Focus

Choose one of your ideas – and it really doesn't matter which one, you'll have time for them all – and do it thoroughly and to the best of your ability. You'll find the satisfaction you get from focusing will be very rewarding.

COLLECT
YOUR IDEAS
FOR
THE FUTURE

3. HOW DO I KNOW WHAT I WANT?

Even if we know something isn't right in our lives, we don't always know what the problem is and what we really want to do about it.

Start noticing

Start by asking yourself, "What's the best thing that happened today?" Then try asking yourself every day or even every hour, "What's the best thing that happened to me in the last hour?" You'll soon start becoming aware of what's going on in your life. Once you start noticing what's good about your life, it'll help you know what you want on a day-to-day level. Then you can focus on putting those good things into your life.

WHAT'S BEEN THE BEST THING ABOUT TODAY?

4. CAN I FOCUS ON A GREAT FUTURE?

Start realizing your big vision for the future by creating a simple picture showing what you want.

Find a picture of your future

If you have a big vision (p24) and know that in five years' time you want to become a DJ or work as a vet, make a picture of yourself doing just that. Find a picture of someone living the life you want to live, then cut out a photo of your head and stick it where that person's head is.

Every time you don't know what to do next, look at the picture you created of yourself in the future and think what you could be doing to get there. The "Future You" will help you know the next step to take.

USE PICTURES TO HELP YOU FOCUS

5. CAN I FOCUS ON GETTING WHAT I WANT?

Once you have a sense of purpose you'll know what you want to achieve and you can focus on it.

Before going on stage an actor knows the role they are going to perform. They know what happens in each scene. It's the the audience that has no idea of the ending. If you know where you want to go in your life, you can start steering each scene towards that place.

Focus on results

Before you start anything – a phone call, a trip, a lesson or a meeting – ask yourself, "What do I want to get out of this in terms of my big vision?" This will make you focus on what you're going to do and will help you achieve the outcome you want.

KNOW WHAT YOU WANT OUT OF EACH SCENE OF YOUR LIFE

6. HOW CAN I THINK POSITIVELY?

If you think negative thoughts, you feel negative. If you think positive thoughts, you feel positive.

Daydreaming

There is a really good way of focusing on the future which you already use. It's called daydreaming, using your imagination or visualizing. Most of us do it all the time, but not always positively. You may imagine the person you fancy ignoring you or you may imagine arriving at a party wearing the wrong clothes and everyone laughing at you. The technique is right, only you need to flip it round.

Daydream positively

From now on, focus on positive scenarios. Have you ever imagined playing a game of football with a sports coach watching you and picking you for the team; or acting in a play and getting a standing ovation?

Two successful ways to imagine

There are two main ways of imagining: process and result. You can choose which way suits you best and then start.

Either way, make your imaginings as full as you can – bring in all the senses (sight, sound, touch, taste and smell). Daydream whenever you can. It will really help you focus on what you want to achieve. One way of imagining will work more naturally for you than the other. Some of us like starting in the present and slowly imagining the future – "process imagining". Others are happier starting with a dream and working out how to achieve it – "result imagining".

1. Process

Process imagining is when you go through the activity from beginning to end. Let's say you want to run faster. The process way is to imagine yourself getting ready for a run, starting it, imagine actually running – really feeling your body and how it's moving – and then finishing the run.

2. Result

Result imagining starts with the result and then rewinds. Again, let's use the example that you want to run faster. You imagine yourself winning the race, you hear the applause, see everyone congratulating you and really get into how it feels to win that race – then work backwards to how you did it.

JAMES'S STORY

James was going for an interview in a few weeks' time and was pretty nervous about it. Every day, a few times a day, he would go through the interview in his mind. He thought about what he would wear, he imagined how the interview would work depending on how many interviewers there were. James went through everything really thoroughly – how long he would pause before answering a question, how he'd stand so he looked confident, about the kind of handshake he'd give, about all the different kinds of questions they might ask him and how he'd answer them and about what he'd ask them. James also imagined leaving with a big smile, thanking everyone who was there. By the time he went along for his interview he felt pretty good – and, needless to say, the interviewers were impressed, too. James got the job.

YOUR MIND
WILL INSPIRE
YOUR
FUTURE

7. WHAT DO I DO IF

> **Concentrate all your thoughts upon the work at hand. The sun's rays do not burn until brought to a focus.**
>
> Alexander Graham Bell

Sometimes life happens and you get interrupted, whether it's the phone, an e-mail or a real life disturbance. If you're focusing on something and get interrupted it can take a while to refocus. You may even find that you no longer have time to write that report. You now have to regain your focus.

Where's your focus now?

Each time you get distracted, focus again by asking yourself, "What's the most important thing I could be doing/talking about/thinking about right now?" Then do it. Just that one simple question will refocus you.

I CAN'T FOCUS?

WHAT'S
THE MOST
IMPORTANT USE
OF YOUR TIME
RIGHT NOW?

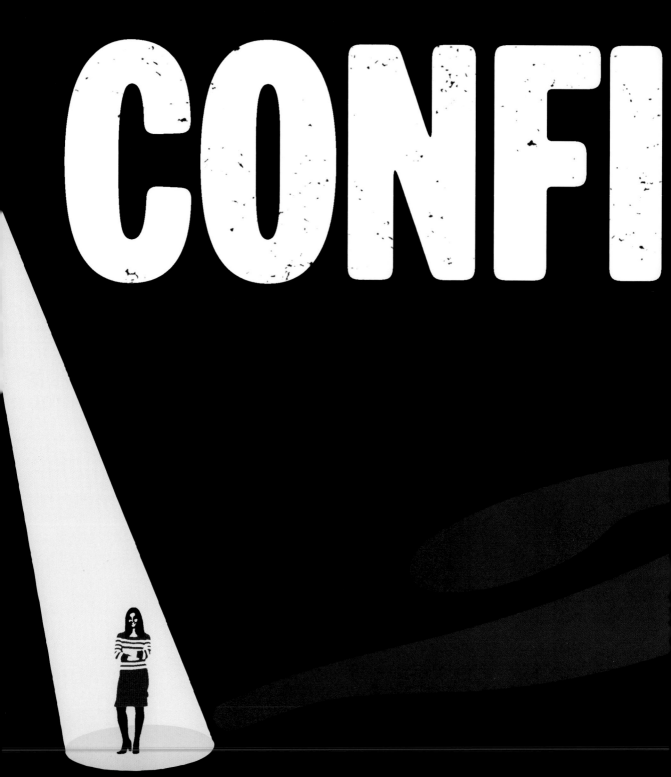

DENCE

> **"Nobody can make you feel inferior without your consent."**
>
> Eleanor Roosevelt

Eleanor Roosevelt knew what she was talking about. Imagine someone criticized the way you tied your shoelaces. They taunted you, made fun of you. Would you feel inferior? No.

Whenever we feel really confident about something – like our ability to tie our shoelaces – we know we're good. We feel really secure about ourselves and our skills. But can you remember back to first learning how to tie those shoelaces? It sounded and felt so complicated and awkward, but you mastered it.

We can learn confidence. We can learn never to give our consent to feeling inferior.

"Thousands of geniuses live and die undiscovered – either by themselves or by others."
Mark Twain

1. HOW

It's simple. A great way to start becoming more confident is to notice everything you're achieving and give yourself credit for it.

Create an achievements list

You achieve things all the time, but often you might not notice them. It doesn't matter how large or how small your achievement is, just keep focusing on what you have done and write it down. Your list could have things in it like:

- I made a phone call I was dreading.
- I started to learn Photoshop.
- I finished the book I was reading.
- I cooked my first perfect fried egg.

Achievements create confidence

If the things you're achieving are things that you felt unsure about to start with, so much the better. The more risk that's involved, the greater the sense of achievement you'll get and the more confident you'll become. If you can do something you're dreading every day or at least every week, you'll notice how quickly your confidence will grow – and how much you're achieving.

DO I LEARN CONFIDENCE?

EVERYTHING YOU DO WILL BUILD YOUR CONFIDENCE

It is the expectation of success or failure that determines your confidence and therefore your behaviour. If you think you're going to have problems with an exam, you probably will. If you think you're going to find the exam easy, you probably will.

Change your thoughts

You can train your mind to think whatever you want it to think, so long as you keep that thought precise and clear. Luckily, your brain is easily persuaded. It won't happen overnight – they say it takes three weeks for a thought to become fixed in your mind, but there's nothing to stop you starting right now.

What do you want to think?

Before you start training your mind, decide what thoughts you want to have in it. Begin by finding a statement that would be great if you believed in it. The more "unlike" you it feels at first, the better. Here are a few ideas:

- I have lots of friends.
- I get on well with everyone.
- I'm incredibly intelligent.
- I'm great at exams.
- I'm really handsome/beautiful.
- I have a great body.
- I'm great at making money.
- I'm super healthy (if you want to give up a habit that's bad for your health).

You can choose to think anything. Make your new thought something you really want and that matches these four criteria:

1. It has to be short.
2. It has to be in the present tense.
3. It has to be in the first person.
4. It has to be positive.

If you find you have negative thoughts of yourself, decide to think the opposite.

Training your mind

Once you've chosen your statement, repeat it several times a day, like a mantra. For example, you might want to say it every time you see a mirror or every time you go to the bathroom. The more times you can say it, the more chance it has of working. And, each time you say it, imagine you really believe it – until you do.

You might be the kind of person who waits for others to boost your confidence by saying you look great or that you make them feel good. But you don't have to wait. You can be your own best friend. Rather than let somebody else get you down and make you feel inferior, know you're great.

TINA'S STORY

Even though Tina was pretty good at everything she did, she never really rated herself. She didn't think she was particularly good-looking and she didn't think she was particularly bright and she didn't like her hair or her figure and she didn't think people really liked her. To cut a long story short, Tina felt under-confident.

One day, Tina decided that instead of thinking, "I'm rubbish", she'd do something about it. She chose a sentence, "I am confident – I can do anything I want" and for three weeks repeated it in front of the mirror in the morning, in the middle of the day and at night. Every time Tina said her sentence, she looked at herself in the mirror and although at first she felt slightly ridiculous, she said it with as much commitment and conviction as she could. And what was incredible was that very soon Tina began to believe her sentence. Her confidence grew, she started going out more with her friends, talking more in groups and generally just feeling much, much better about herself. And, of course, the better she felt, the more she did and then she became more confident and did more and on and on it went – a really positive loop. Tina's statement had worked and soon she didn't need to say her sentence any more.

YOU ARE WHAT YOU THINK

3. WHAT COULD MAKE ME FEEL LESS NERVOUS?

Do you remember when you used to play dare games. You might have felt really scared, had butterflies in your stomach, sweaty palms, a dry throat and yet, once you'd done your dare, you felt on top of the world.

Dare yourself all the time

In a way you get more confident by daring yourself to do things you otherwise wouldn't. And the more scared you are before you do something, the more your confidence will grow once you've done it – even if you don't succeed.

Jump and the net will appear

You could start talking to yourself like this:

- *I dare myself to ask her out.*
- *I dare myself not to be nervous in tests.*
- *I dare myself to talk to someone I don't know at the next party I go to.*
- *I dare myself not to worry about what I'm wearing.*
- *I dare myself to say "No" when my neighbours next ask me to babysit.*

By daring yourself over and over again, sooner or later you'll realize that it has stopped being a dare and become something you can actually do.

The only thing that will make you feel less nervous is practise. Do something over and over and over again and when you start to get blasé about doing it, you'll know you're no longer nervous. If it helps, ask a friend to help you. You can practise anything – from walking into a room with your head held high, to cooking the perfect dish for a party, or rock climbing.

THEO'S STORY

Theo was really nervous about exams. He'd always dreaded them. Although he was often near the top of the class, when he came to a timed paper he got totally flustered and couldn't think straight. As his final exams got nearer and nearer he was in a real state and unable to see how he could pass them. One of his friends suggested he go and talk to a teacher about this, which Theo sensibly did. The teacher decided that the way through his barriers was to practise. Every day, for three weeks, Theo sat a mock exam and dared himself to keep calm while doing it. At first he was nervous and his results were appalling, but he slowly got better and better. By the day of Theo's first exam he was completely calm and sailed through.

4. HOW CAN I STOP THINKING MYSELF SMALL?

YOU ARE NOT CLEVER ENOUGH

YOU CAN'T DO THAT!

you are NOT loveable

It's not entirely your fault, but let's say you're a pretty large factor in why you feel under-confident.

It's all to do with those voices inside your head saying things such as:
- *You can't do that!*
- *You're not clever enough!*
- *You're not loveable!*

These voices stop you feeling you can do anything. And yet, once you know what you really want to do, the actions themselves are usually quite straightforward. Focusing on these will move you on. As you dare yourself to do things you'll notice how every action shows one of those beliefs is wrong and can be got rid of.

Are these voices you?

Listen carefully to all these voices and what they're saying. You've probably had them in your head since you were young.

Make a list of all of them and think about where they came from. Was it from your family, teachers or friends? Or did you make them up when you compared yourself to others and come up with your own conclusions?

Contradict those voices

Once you start noticing all the ways you're thinking yourself small, you can contradict those thoughts and slowly get rid of them. It's a matter of noticing that they're no longer accurate. It may seem like hard work to notice them – there can be so many – but don't give up. They're just your beliefs, not reality.

Let's imagine you want to score a goal in a football match and that voice has just started, "You can't score goals, you never score one". Because you've become aware of what's happening and have actually noticed that voice starting, you could consciously contradict it and say, "Yes I can". Then see if you can remember a recent achievement and concentrate on that.

ARE YOUR THOUGHTS BELIEFS OR FACTS?

5. HOW CAN I THINK BIG?

Whatever you think affects the things you do. If you think small, you won't do much. If you think big, you'll start achieving.

The under-confident loop

Your thoughts keep you small and then your small actions make your thoughts even smaller.

TOM'S STORY

Example 1

Tom wanted to win the long-distance race that was taking place in a few months' time, but he kept thinking, "I'm not fit enough", "I'm not determined enough", "I haven't got enough time to practise". Tom's thoughts were so under-confident that he decided not to run the race and didn't start training for it. He didn't even apply. Instead his thoughts grew even more negative, "I'm not good enough", "I'm a failure", "I can never do anything".

The think big loop

Your thoughts can help you achieve and then your achievements help to grow your thoughts.

TOM'S STORY

Example 2

Tom wanted to win the long-distance race that was taking place in a few months' time and thought of all the reasons why it might be possible for him to win. "I am a great runner", "I have a lot of will-power", "I have a good support system". He felt good about his chances and signed up for the race, telling everyone what he was doing. At the same time he started training and soon started achieving results. He kept on training, ran the race and, although he didn't win, he completed it and broke his own personal record. That felt great and, as a result, Tom's mind stepped up a gear, "I'm so good", "I can achieve anything". The next race he applied for was even longer.

Take small actions

Small, forward-moving actions can make a big difference.

TOM'S STORY

Example 3

Tom wanted to win the long-distance race that was taking place in a few months' time, but he kept thinking, "I'm not fit enough", "I'm not determined enough", "I haven't got enough time to practise". Although Tom was under-confident he decided to give it a go anyway – the first few things he had to do were easy after all. He signed up for the race, telling everyone what he was doing – and that was easy. At the same time he started training, which was also easy. Soon Tom started achieving results and at the same time his mindset started to change. Instead of, "I'm not fit enough", he said, "I can get fit enough". Instead of "I'm not determined enough", he started thinking, "I will do it". By taking one step at a time, Tom was able to turn his negative thoughts into positive ones.

Decide which loop is for you

When you know you want to do something, think about which loop you're in right now and which loop you'd like to be in.

ACTIONS CHANGE THOUGHTS

6. WHAT IF I FAIL?

WHEN YOU FEEL CONFIDENT YOU DON'T EVEN THINK ABOUT FAILURE.

If you follow famous people in the papers, you'll see they often get things wrong. They may lose money on an idea or they may release a song that flops. They don't stop and give up. They are confident enough to learn from their experience about what not to do next time.

Confidence helps you feel in control

Feeling confident is being positive and realistic about yourself and your situation. It's feeling in control. You're not showing off about how brilliantly you're going to do something, you're just calmly doing it. Think of the things you feel confident about – don't you just get on and do them?

Failure isn't an issue

If you're feeling confident and something goes wrong, you see it as a learning experience and remain positive about yourself. You just try again.

We often assume that we have to do everything "right" and yet if you think about your best friend or brothers or sisters and the times they've done something "wrong" have you minded? You probably forgive them everything and allow them to "fail". You love them as they are. Now, like those famous people, love yourself as you are – "failures" and all.

HASSAN'S STORY
Example 1
Hassan failed his driving theory test. He exaggerated wildly as he berated himself: "I'm always bad at passing things", "I'll never pass my theory test or my driving test", "I wasn't meant to drive". He believed all these angry thoughts and started feeling he was a total failure. It was months before Hassan plucked up the courage to get behind the wheel again.

HASSAN'S STORY
Example 2
Hassan failed his driving theory test and felt a little shaken. Looking back he could see how he could learn from his failure. He'd been a bit complacent about revising – and he hadn't driven for a few weeks so hadn't been thinking about the road. He got straight on the phone and booked his retake. At the same time he marked out an hour every evening in which to do his revision thoroughly.

BEING CONFIDENT ALLOWS YOU TO FAIL

7. WHY DON'T I ALWAYS FEEL GOOD ABOUT MYSELF?

Confidence fluctuates depending on what's going on in your life. You can feel more or less confident and there may be times that the downs feel overwhelming and your confidence dives down too.

Stuff happens

Down times often happen if you "fail" in any way. It might be when you get dumped, lose your job or mess up a test. These down times can even happen if you're asked to do something really challenging that you feel you might fail at. Mostly these feelings of gloominess and under-confidence are to do with being at the mercy of someone else and feeling out of control or powerless.

It's OK to be sad

Maybe you want a bit of sadness right now. That's OK. It's fine to be sad. Maybe you're tired. That's not OK – go to bed. Maybe you're putting yourself down and allowing your negative thoughts to make you feel gloomy and under-confident. That's not OK either. Work out why you're putting yourself down and decide if that's really what you want to do. If you don't, stop it.

Three ways of getting through low confidence periods

You can do each of these singly or together. The more determined you are to get through your period of under-confidence, the faster you'll be able to turn it around.

1. Start training your mind

Using mental acrobatics (p58) will slowly begin to make you feel more positive about yourself. Find a statement that will work to build up your confidence.

2. Do something you like

Bring out your achievements list (p152) and do something that you know will instantly make you feel better – something you're confident about doing well. It could be strumming your guitar, kicking a ball around, calling a friend. As your confidence slowly builds up you can take bigger and bigger steps towards changing the situation.

3. Focus on the good

Keep focusing on all the good things that are happening – no matter how small they are (p47). Think about everything that you're achieving and let yourself off the hook.

IT'S OK TO BE SAD SOMETIMES

8. WHY WOULD ANYONE WANT TO BE UNDER-CONFIDENT?

Being under-confident can be quite cosy. There are advantages to being under-confident and that's what keeps you in your comfort zone.

What advantages are there?

Here are just a few reasons why you might want to stay under-confident:

- You won't be expected to do anything new (so you can't "fail").
- You don't have to take responsibility for yourself – instead you get looked after.
- You might have lots of people being supportive and gentle to you and sympathizing with you, "Don't worry, I failed my theory test too".
- You don't have to come across like an over-confident show-off – even though those people are often not really confident people, they're just pretending.

All of these advantages are stopping you from taking risks and becoming confident. If you want to start feeling more self-assured, a good thing to do is to identify the advantages you're getting from your under-confidence and find other ways of getting them.

Really confident people don't need to show off; they don't think there's anything special about their abilities. Do you show off in the areas you feel confident in?

GEORGE'S STORY

George had no confidence with computers. When his computer went wrong he'd have a tantrum, feel out of control and cry help until someone came along to fix it for him. Then George realized that the advantages of being under-confident and helpless around computers were that he'd have an excuse to invite his friends round. His lack of computer knowledge was a social tool. Once George understood this, he decided to learn about computers. Instead of crying help he'd simply invite his friends round – he didn't need to be helpless any more.

THERE ARE ADVANTAGES TO BEING UNDER-CONFIDENT

9. HOW CAN I SOUND

MORE CONFIDENT?

So many people apologize for themselves all the time. Maybe you don't want to come across as a show-off, but you don't want to downplay your talents either.

Downplaying your talents may make you feel wonderfully modest, but ultimately saying out loud to yourself (and others) that you're good at something is far better than putting yourself down.

Rewriting your qualities

Rewrite expressions you use so you don't sound less capable than you really are.

Present statement: *I'm quite good at sport*.
Ideal statement: *I play rugby really well*.
Present statement: *I do OK at school*.
Ideal statement: *I'm at the top of the class*.

TALK YOURSELF UP RATHER THAN DOWN

10. HOW CAN I BE MORE CONFIDENT?

Imagine being somebody else

If you've got something coming up that you're dreading a little – like going to a party on your own when you might not know many people or going to an interview – there's a fun game that can help you get into the right frame of mind.

Choose someone

Imagine someone else could go to the party or the interview for you. Who would you like that someone to be? James Bond? Madonna? Your favourite teacher? Your best friend?

Once you've chosen someone you'd like to be there instead of you, imagine you are them. Get into their head as best as you can and answer these questions:

- What does XXX believe about him/herself and life?
- How do you feel as XXX?
- How do you look as XXX?
- How would XXX see the party or interview?
- What thoughts would be running through their head?
- What might you say as XXX?

How does this work?

You won't instantly become that person, but just by thinking differently – as if you were them – you'll find you know things that wouldn't otherwise occur to you and that you'll start behaving in a way you wouldn't normally behave. Plus you'll have some of their confidence – a good stand-by until you've got your own.

For the future...

Once you've got your own confidence, go through the questions being yourself. How good does that feel?

11. HOW CAN I BUILD MY CONFIDENCE?

There are times when, without even thinking about it, you'll find yourself in difficult situations. They may be new problems or something you've never experienced before.

You've been here before

Instead of panicking or worrying about a problem, simply ask yourself, "What helped me through before?" Remember what you did and which of your qualities helped you to do it. Then think about how you can apply those qualities right now.

Trust your intuition

You actually know more that you think you do, so instead of relying on your head, start listening to your heart. Learn that your intuition often knows the answer even if you don't think you do. If something doesn't feel right, ask yourself what your gut feeling is. Keep trusting how you feel about yourself, about your work, about your friends, about your family. Once you know you can trust yourself you will feel more confident.

12. IS IT OK TO
TIME

Being alone is great if you're comfortable with it.

Being happy on your own is a huge skill, especially as it means you don't need to worry whether you're liked or not. Ironically, once everyone can see how you don't need them, you'll be the person they all want to be with.

What will others think of me?

You'll never really know what anyone else thinks of you. Plus each friend will think something different, depending on who they are and what they're like. The only thing you can do is be happy with yourself and think about whether you like them.

Do I like them?

Rather than worrying if friends like you, flip the question around and ask yourself:
- *How do I know if I like them?*
- *How do they know if I like them?*

MAKE A LIST OF ALL THE THINGS YOU'RE OK ABOUT DOING ALONE.

SPEND ALONE?

13. HOW CAN I FEEL CONFIDEN

IN A RELATIONSHIP?

❝To say 'I love you' one must first be able to say the 'I'.❞

Ayn Rand

14. HOW CAN I FEEL HAPPIER ABOUT MY BODY?

Most of us feel under-confident about one bit of our body or another. There are many different ways you can start to become more comfortable about your body.

Remember compliments

Start by thinking about all the bits you do like – the bits that maybe you've been complimented on – and see how you can focus on those. Each of us has something, whether it's expressive eyes or a commanding presence. Become aware of your strength and keep building on it. If it's your expressive eyes, relax your face more and smile. If it's your commanding presence, allow yourself to stand tall, but incorporate friendly gestures to show you are open to communication.

Think positive

Study photos and films of yourself with a positive viewpoint. Instead of criticizing the way you look, notice all the good things until you can see and believe them.

Use your body to give you confidence

Here are seven ways you can use your body to make you feel more confident about yourself (see also p89):

1. Smiling can make you feel and appear more relaxed and confident.

2. Standing up straight will make you look and feel better.

3. Looking up – even for a split second – rather than at the floor, will give you confidence.

4. A steady gaze will make you look confident and then you'll begin to feel it.

5. A relaxed body will make it difficult for you to feel nervous or anxious. Notice where you are holding tension and relax your body.

6. Open (rather than crossed) arms and legs will make you feel less of an outsider.

7. Dancing or any sport can make you feel more energetic and happier.

How will I know if I'm good at sex?

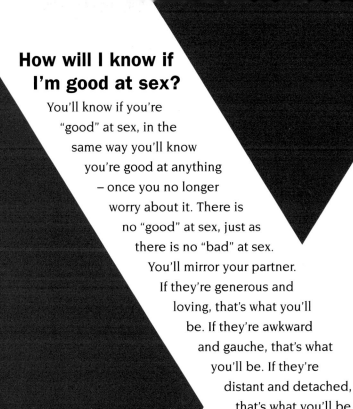

You'll know if you're "good" at sex, in the same way you'll know you're good at anything – once you no longer worry about it. There is no "good" at sex, just as there is no "bad" at sex. You'll mirror your partner. If they're generous and loving, that's what you'll be. If they're awkward and gauche, that's what you'll be. If they're distant and detached, that's what you'll be. And conversely, if you're feeling comfortable and enjoying yourself they will be, too. Enjoyable sex is about laughter and love and trust and being relaxed. If you're with someone who's fun, relaxed and loving out of bed, then you'll be the same with them in bed.

IGNORE THE WAY YOUR BODY LOOKS, FEEL THE WAY IT IS

> **"The problem with communication ... is the illusion that it has been accomplished."**
> George Bernard Shaw

There are so many ways in which we communicate – phone, email, text – and although these are great for speed and efficiency, in order to feel any real connection with anyone, it is vital to be face to face.

If you're with someone you can pick up what they want to say by looking at their eyes, observing their expressions and their body language. You'll see what they really mean. We all know communication is about talking, but it's as much, if not more, about listening – really hearing someone else and knowing you are being heard.

1. WHAT CAN I DO TO MAKE

Ever felt no one is listening to you? Do you feel you've said something and no one has got it? It is said that the reason we have two ears and one mouth is because it's twice as difficult to listen as to talk. This can be true.

Why don't people listen?

Often people don't listen to you because they've got so many interesting or exciting thoughts of their own running through their heads. Thoughts like:

- I have a story that's better than this.
- I can solve their problem.
- I wonder what's on at the cinema tonight.
- I'd love to tell this great joke I just heard.

Show them how to listen

If you're not being listened to, you'll have to be a good listener for your friends so that they can understand how it's done. Not only will they learn from you how to listen properly, but they'll feel heard and will be more likely to listen to you in return. Even if they don't, you'll know you've given them your best. Think about your friends too – if they never listen, are they really the ones you want?

Working it out

Sometimes simply by talking for a few minutes uninterrupted to a friend, family member or even a stranger, you can solve your own problems.

PEOPLE LISTEN TO ME?

Demonstrate you're listening

When you're listening to someone, gently repeat back what you've heard them say. Also try to include what you thought they felt. They'll know that you really did hear them and that you're there for them. You can say things such as:

- "I'm really pleased. You sound over the moon. I know you've wanted to go out with him for ages."
- "You mean you got that guitar you showed me? I can hear how excited you are. When can I hear you play it?"

Get listening...

With a friend or member of your family, set a timer for five minutes and take it in turns to spend that five minutes talking. If the timer feels a little forced, maybe go and get some coffee or go to the pub and whoever buys the drinks earns the chance to do the talking first. If it's your turn to talk, ask the other person to listen to you without interrupting, just occasionally summing up what you have been saying and guessing at how you might be feeling. If they want to, they can ask you a question or two. After five minutes, swap, and you listen. After the ten minutes is up, have a chat about how you felt listening and being listened to. This will show you both how rewarding it is to listen to others and how much both of you can get out of it.

LISTENING IS MORE POWERFUL THAN YOU THINK

2. ARE SOME QUESTIONS BETTER THAN OTHERS?

Does she have no taste?

Do I look horrible?

Does no one like me?

WHY DOESN'T SHE LIKE ME?

WHAT COULD I DO TO MAKE HER LIKE ME?

Make her laugh.

Take her to the cinema.

Listen to her.

When you were a small child, you probably asked "Why?" all the time.

> **Why are you my brother?**
> **Why do girls have breasts?**
> **Why are you reading a book?**

As you get older, you'll carry on doing this.

> **Why doesn't my computer work?**
> **Why don't you phone them?**
> **Why do I feel so bad?**

This kind of question is fine, especially if your computer really is broken, but it's not so great if you really want to know what's going on.

Why "Why?" doesn't work

Imagine you have a problem to solve, like you've got an exam in a week's time and you're not revising or there's a girl you fancy and you don't think she fancies you.

If you ask:
Why aren't I starting my revision?
the answers might be something like:

• I don't know where to start
• I can't be bothered
• I haven't left enough time

If, on the other hand you ask:
What could I do to start my revision?
the answers might be more like:

• I could make a timetable

• I could ask a friend to help
• I could start with the bits I've forgotten

Similarly, if you ask:
Why doesn't she like me?
the answers will be something like:

• Because I'm horrible
• Because she's got no taste
• Because no one likes me

If, on the other hand, you ask:
What could I do to make her like me?
the answers will be something like:

• I could be funny when I'm around her
• I could listen to her stories
• I could ask her to a film I know she wants to see

A different sort of question

"Why" questions are useful when there's something technical to be solved, but they can make you feel guilty or frustrated. Instead, if you word your questions using "What?" or "How?" you could find an answer. These questions are called "outcome" questions, because they demand an outcome. They help access deeper feelings and bring your intuition to the fore. They're powerful and can lead to great conversations.

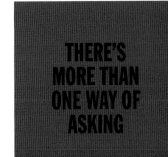

THERE'S MORE THAN ONE WAY OF ASKING

3. I OFTEN FEEL I DON'T KNOW THE ANSWER, WHAT SHOULD I DO?

When you're asked a question, you'll often reply, "I don't know". But you do.

Every time you're about to reply, "I don't know", stop. Simply ask yourself, "If I knew the answer what would I say?" You'll be amazed at the answers your intuition comes up with. Trust that you know the answer.

YOU KNOW MORE THAN YOU THINK

4. WHAT IS MY

Approximately 7% of communication is made up of the actual words you say, 38% is to do with your voice (tone, speed, volume, pitch) and 55% is visual (eye contact and body language). So what your body says is the most important bit.

Your body is a giveaway as to how you're feeling. If you're relaxed, your body will be stretched out, comfortable and confident. If you're tense or nervous or maybe even defensive your body will be closed up with crossed arms and legs.

BODY SAYING ABOUT ME?

Get comfortable with your body

If you're comfortable with yourself others will see you as confident and relaxed. Have a go at relaxing physically. (See also p80)

Get rid of tension

Swing your arms and legs and take big steps, noticing how your body feels.

Take three deep breaths.

Dance (or stretch).

Repeat the word "open" in your head a few times. Your body will start to relax.

Show someone you're listening

It's one thing to listen, another to show someone you're actively listening.

Show you're listening

Uncross your body so neither your arms nor legs are crossed.

Keep your body turned towards the person talking.

Keep your shoulders relaxed.

Look into their eyes, even when they're looking down so that your eyes are there for them when they look up again.

USE YOUR BODY TO ENHANCE YOUR PRESENCE

5. DO FRIENDS INFLUENCE THE WAY I TALK?

You've probably noticed how you say things differently depending on who you're with. It's almost as if you are lots of different people.

Your vocabulary changes, your body language changes and even your voice can change. Most of us change our persona in some way and that's fine until it starts complicating your life. It goes wrong if you find you don't want groups of friends to meet – or even one person from one group to meet one person from another.

Are you becoming someone else?

Take it as a warning sign if you start being so influenced by someone that you're turning into them – especially if you don't like the person you're turning into. It might mean that this friend or group is the wrong person or group for you to be hanging out with right now. Think about who you are and realize that you're great as you are. Being you is the best thing you can do for yourself.

MAGGIE'S STORY

Maggie was reasonably happy going out with Alex until she realized that whenever she was with him she became really whiny. Thinking about it, Maggie was surprised because she wasn't like that with anyone else. One day when they were hanging out at Alex's house, Maggie listened to his mother with amazement. Alex's mum was that whiny person Alex was pushing Maggie into becoming. She decided to end the relationship.

YOU'RE
GREAT
AS YOU
ARE

Often when we want people to like us, we think we have to be witty or fun or good-looking or outrageous, but sometimes all we have to do is listen.

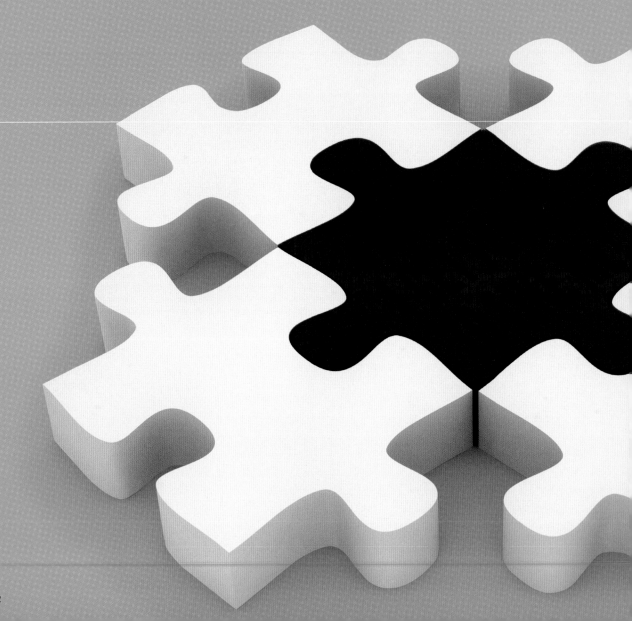

It doesn't cost anything to listen and it means a lot to the person we are listening to. Once you've listened, you can show them how witty, fun, good-looking and outrageous you really are, or can be, but sometimes simply listening and asking them about themselves is the best way to make a friend.

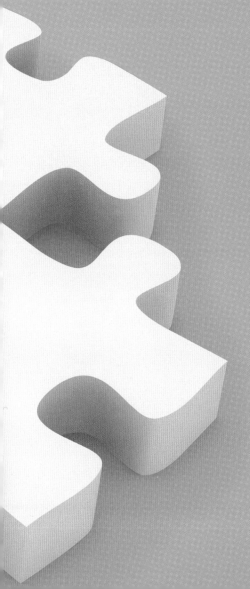

What outcome do you want?

Be clear about your objectives. Do you just want them to like you or do you want something else from them, for example a job, a good degree, to go out with them, or to get some sponsorship money for the run you're doing?

Put yourself in their shoes

Who is the person that you want to like you? Whether it is your tutor, an interviewer or a potential new friend, find out about them. What are they interested in, what sort of language do they use? Research them and then think about what they know about you already and what they might need to know.

Be yourself

Rather than worry about other people liking you, work on who you think you are and be as confident as you can about yourself. The more you like yourself and don't need others, the more they'll like you. Ironic, isn't it?

THINK
ABOUT
OTHERS

7. WHAT CAN I DO TO CHANGE PEOPLE?

You can never change anyone else, you can only change yourself. You can let others know that you'd prefer things to be different, but if you're fed up, it may mean you changing, rather than them.

It's often helpful to let others know what's bothering you, or it can build up in your mind and become more of a problem than it actually is. At the same time, it's important to be tactful in your feedback so that you don't hurt them or make them do something that makes you even crosser.

Think about outcomes

When you want to give feedback, always think first about what outcome you want. If it's to change them, forget it. If it's to let them know you're angry, forget it. If it's to find a compromise, go for it. You may find that just by thinking of the outcome you want, you'll realize there's no need to have that conversation.

For example, let's say your mum always wants you to do stuff for her. Carefully, using feedback, you can help her understand your situation so she will leave you to get on with your own life. Before you start the conversation, make sure you're alone – giving negative feedback in front of others is never a good idea.

The technique described below is called the "feedback sandwich". It's putting something nasty in the middle of two nice things. It may feel a little manipulative, but it's a great communication skill and situations get changed without anyone feeling too aggrieved.

Three tips for giving negative feedback

1. Make it about you, not them

Remember that if you find someone selfish or annoying or irritating in any way, it's the way you see them – it's your point of view and your problem. Everyone else might be perfectly happy with the way they are.

If you say: "You're so…" it makes it about them. If you say: "I find you so…" or "Sometimes I find you a little…" it makes it about you.

Tone it down and make sure that as much as possible they can see it's your problem, rather than theirs.

2. Be specific rather than general

When you're giving someone feedback and letting them know what you feel, be as specific as you can, rather than general, so they really know what you're angry about.

Let them know why you're upset. If you generalize and say, "I find you selfish/annoying", they will want to know why and the conversation that follows may just aggravate the situation rather than calm it down.

If you're very specific, solutions can be found: "I find you selfish when you borrow my clothes without asking" or "I find you annoying when you tell Mum what I've done" makes the problem clear.

3. Don't exaggerate

It's really unhelpful to say someone is "always" something or "never" something. Both are exaggerations and will make the person you're giving the feedback to feel defensive and powerless. They will probably start attacking you back.

Sometimes when you're upset, it's because someone's behaviour is somehow mirroring yours. So, before you give feedback, check out what it is that's at the heart of the problem.

For example, if you feel someone is being really bossy and it's annoying you, think about what it is that's really annoying you about it.

- Is it that they're too controlling?
- Is it that they sound like they're giving out orders?
- Is it that they are too opinionated?
- Is it that they think they're the leader?
- Is it that you like being the boss?

IS IT THEM YOU WANT TO CHANGE, OR YOU?

"Kind words can be short and easy to speak, but their echoes are truly endless."

Mother Teresa

8. HOW IMPORTANT IS IT TO SAY NICE THINGS TO PEOPLE?

It's very important to say nice things to people. It makes them feel good and you will feel good, too.

Praise them

When you want to give someone a compliment, make it about them. So, instead of saying, "I like your smile," say, "You've got such a great smile". Or, instead of saying, "I think you're good at maths," say, "You're so good at maths". Take yourself out of the compliment. Give a compliment every day and see how it makes you feel.

9. WHY DO I FIND COMPLIMENTS

Many of us feel inhibited about compliments. It can feel awkward to give them and embarrassing to receive them.

Yet the wonderful thing about compliments is that they're something you can give someone for free. Once you get used to it, it becomes really easy to say, "What a cool t-shirt" or "Nice shoes" or even, "I hear you've got a fit girlfriend".

Enjoy being complimented

Receiving compliments can be difficult and it's easy to dismiss them. If someone compliments you about your nice eyes it's easy to reply, "They're just a dishwater colour," or about your jumper, "I've had it for years". How do you think that makes them feel? It sort of snubs them and ignoring the compliment altogether is an even harsher rejection.

Learn from compliments

Getting compliments can teach you such a lot about yourself. Compliments can show you what people value and appreciate about you, which is useful to know and confidence boosting.

SO DIFFICULT?

Why do I reject compliments?

One of the main reasons you might ignore compliments is that you feel you're not worth them. The more self-confident you are, the easier you'll find it to accept them. If you find yourself being embarrassed and awkward about receiving a compliment, ask yourself what makes you feel so embarrassed. Don't you feel worth it? Allow yourself to believe you're good. Make a list of all the compliments you've ever received and believe them. Allow them to build your confidence.

How to take a compliment

Smile

Say "Thank you"

Enjoy it

Allow yourself to really take it in

Believe it

Remember it

I READ YOUR BLOG, IT'S GREAT.

THANK YOU, I ENJOYED WRITING IT.

WELL DONE FOR WINNING THE RACE.

ENJOY EACH AND EVERY COMPLIMENT

10. WHY CAN'T I SAY "NO"? HOW OFTEN HAVE YOU SAID "YES" WHEN YOU REALLY WANTED TO SAY "NO"?

Often we say "Yes" when we really don't mean it because we are worried we may lose a friend or upset someone. Yet no one minds if you say "No".

Will they feel rejected?

Think about how you feel when someone says, "No" to you.

- Do you mind or do you respect them for having made a decision?
- Do you feel rejected or do you understand that they must have a reason?
- Do you dislike them or admire them for being able to be honest with you?

When you say "No", it's because you really have to (or want to). Most of us don't say "No" just to flex our muscles. We do it because we're tired, or busy, or don't want to do something. And the more we say "No" the more others respect us and know we're people who say what we mean.

Saying "Yes" to you

We're all good at saying "Yes" to other people but sometimes when you do this, you're saying "No" to yourself. What's better is if you can find out what you'd really like to do and then say "Yes" to what you want to do – even if it means saying "No" to someone else.

Imagine yourself as your best friend

We're often much kinder to our best friend than we are to ourselves. So it can help to imagine you're your best friend and to think about what that best friend would like. Imagining yourself as your best friend, is there anyone or anything that you want to say "No" to right now? If so, do it.

If you spend your time doing things you aren't really interested in doing, you won't have any time to do what you do want to do. Make a list of all the things you'd like to say "No" to. Then work out how you can do that.

You may also want to say "No" to all the negative thoughts you have running through your head, like, "I'm no good at music", "I can't get organized", "I'm rubbish at making friends" and so on. Make a list of all of those thoughts you want to say "No" to and start saying "No" to them now.

SAYING "YES"...

and linger in his own company. 🙶

Seneca

We all know people who are organized – think about your school friends or your teachers. They always arrive on time, do their work on time and know where everything is.

Are you organized or does your heart sink just thinking about getting organized? There are many advantages to being organized, not least that you will feel more in control and therefore at peace with yourself. There are also advantages to being disorganized and you'll discover these as you go.

ORGANIZAT

ON

1. IS IT OK TO BE MESSY?

You decide. What amount of tidiness do you want?

If you think about your life – your room, your bag, your clothes, your work, your mobile, your e-mails, your heart, your stomach, your mind – you'll instantly know which bits are working for you and which aren't. A full mind can keep you awake at night. A full bag can mean that you lose your travelcard every day – twice. Heaps of clothes can make you feel like you've got nothing to wear. A full stomach can make you feel heavy and unattractive.

Advantages to mess

There are many reasons not to declutter. Never deleting texts can make you feel important and popular. Keeping your bed unmade may make your room feel more homely. Having full pockets may make you feel that you'll never lose anything. There are always advantages to everything you do.

The same but organized

Tidying up does not mean you have to change. If you feel your image is one of a laid-back, relaxed individual, you can still be that person, but with an organized diary and bedroom, it may make you even more calm and laid-back.

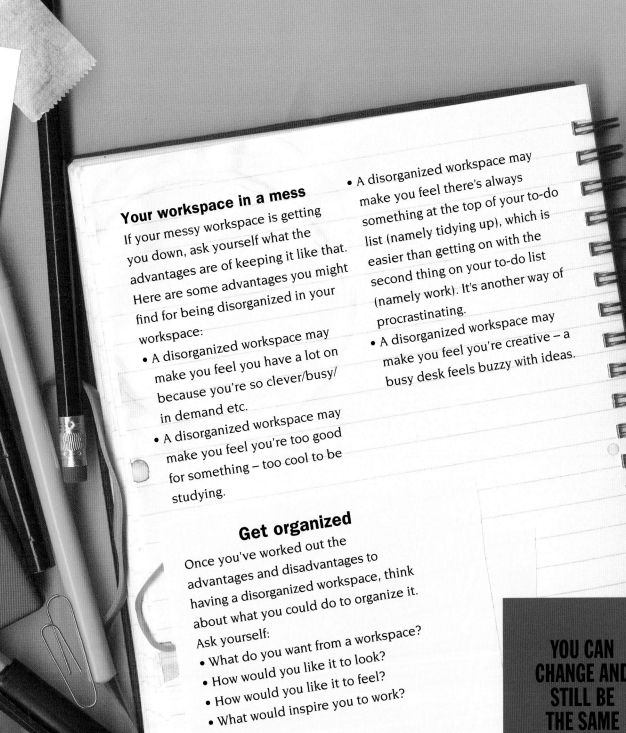

Your workspace in a mess

If your messy workspace is getting you down, ask yourself what the advantages are of keeping it like that. Here are some advantages you might find for being disorganized in your workspace:

- A disorganized workspace may make you feel you have a lot on because you're so clever/busy/ in demand etc.
- A disorganized workspace may make you feel you're too good for something – too cool to be studying.
- A disorganized workspace may make you feel there's always something at the top of your to-do list (namely tidying up), which is easier than getting on with the second thing on your to-do list (namely work). It's another way of procrastinating.
- A disorganized workspace may make you feel you're creative – a busy desk feels buzzy with ideas.

Get organized

Once you've worked out the advantages and disadvantages to having a disorganized workspace, think about what you could do to organize it. Ask yourself:

- What do you want from a workspace?
- How would you like it to look?
- How would you like it to feel?
- What would inspire you to work?

YOU CAN CHANGE AND STILL BE THE SAME

2. HOW CAN I GET MORE DONE?

You can't get more straightforward than the concept of a time sheet.

It's brilliant and you'll probably only have to fill it in for a day (or maybe a week) to see how it works.

Create your time sheet

Take a plain sheet of paper, divide it into seven days (columns) and 24 hours (rows) and, as the week goes on, start filling in what you're doing every single hour of the day. Now, look at what you're spending your time on.

How can you get organized?

Look objectively at your time sheet. How could you get more done? What could you stop doing to give yourself more time to do what you really want to?

ALEX'S STORY

Alex had got a great-sounding guitar for her birthday and wanted to teach herself to play, but there never seemed to be enough time. Alex heard about time sheets and decided to have a go. She was amazed at where her time went. Without really realizing it, she spent about an hour each morning on getting ready, about four hours every night chatting with friends online and on the phone and, at the weekend, about twelve hours a night was spent in bed sleeping. Alex decided to cut down on an hour of social networking every day – three hours was long enough. Alex had created an hour a day to learn guitar in.

HOURS	MONDAY	TUESDAY	WEDNESDAY	THURSDAY	FRIDAY	SATURDAY	SUNDAY
12.00 AM	SLEEP	SLEEP	SLEEP	SLEEP	SLEEP	SLEEP	SLEEP
1.00 AM							
	GETTING READY	GETTING READY	GETTING READY	GETTING READY	GETTING READY		
		COLLEGE	COLLEGE	COLLEGE	COLLEGE	GETTING READY	GETTING READY
						SATURDAY JOB	GETTING READY
							VISIT GRAN
				TENNIS			
				RUNNING			
				MUSIC LESSON			GUITAR PRACTISE
	HOMEWORK	ONLINE	HOMEWORK	ONLINE	VISIT FRIENDS		VISIT FRIENDS
6.00 PM	ONLINE		CALL FRIENDS		CINEMA		
7.00 PM		COOK DINNER	ONLINE			SEEING FRIENDS	REVISION
8.00 PM	DINNER	HOMEWORK					WATCH TV
9.00 PM	READING	ONLINE			ONLINE		ONLINE
10.00 PM				SLEEP		ONLINE	SLEEP
11.00 PM	SLEEP	SLEEP	SLEEP		SLEEP	SLEEP	

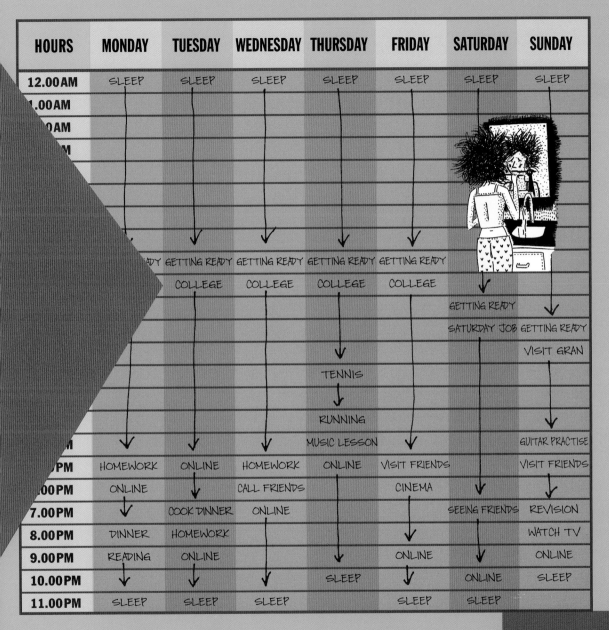

THERE ARE TWENTY-FOUR HOURS TO PLAY WITH

3. WHY DO I

Three reasons for procrastination

Everybody procrastinates, even though it stops them getting on with things that have probably been giving them a guilty conscience for ages.

Procrastination is something you can overcome, so let's think about why you do it and how to get over it.

You may think you procrastinate because you're frightened or undecided, but in fact both of these lead to one of these three reasons.

1. You want to do it perfectly

2. You feel overwhelmed by how much you have to do

3. You're rebelling

It doesn't have to be perfect
There are many things we don't do unless we can do them perfectly. For example, you might not plan a fancy dress party because you're not sure what the perfect theme would be. Perfectionism keeps you stuck.

Just do it
When you get stuck trying to be perfect, the only thing to do is to just start. Invite your friends and choose any theme for the party. You can always change your mind. Trust that you've made the right decision for now.

There's too much...
Sometimes what you want to do just feels too big. You've got a project to complete and you have no idea where to start or how to break it down into manageable bits. Maybe you want to build a website and really don't know how to get going.

Get help
If you feel overwhelmed, ask for help. Invite a friend to start that project with you, or a computer literate friend to help you with the website. There are times when it's all right not to be a hero – or at least not a lone hero.

HOURS	MONDAY	TUESDAY	WEDNESDAY	THURSDAY	FRIDAY	SATURDAY	SUNDAY
12.00 AM	SLEEP	SLEEP	SLEEP	SLEEP	SLEEP	SLEEP	SLEEP
1.00 AM							
2.00 AM							
3.00 AM							
4.00 AM							
5.00 AM							
6.00 AM							
7.00 AM							
8.00 AM	GETTING READY	GETTING READY	GETTING READY	GETTING READY	GETTING READY		
9.00 AM	COLLEGE	COLLEGE	COLLEGE	COLLEGE	COLLEGE	GETTING READY	GETTING READY
10.00 AM						SATURDAY JOB	GETTING READY
11.00 AM							VISIT GRAN
12.00 PM				TENNIS			
1.00 PM							
2.00 PM				RUNNING			
3.00 PM				MUSIC LESSON			GUITAR PRACTISE
4.00 PM	HOMEWORK	ONLINE	HOMEWORK	ONLINE	VISIT FRIENDS		VISIT FRIENDS
5.00 PM	ONLINE		CALL FRIENDS		CINEMA		
6.00 PM							
7.00 PM		COOK DINNER	ONLINE			SEEING FRIENDS	REVISION
8.00 PM	DINNER	HOMEWORK					WATCH TV
9.00 PM	READING	ONLINE			ONLINE		ONLINE
10.00 PM				SLEEP		ONLINE	SLEEP
11.00 PM	SLEEP	SLEEP	SLEEP		SLEEP	SLEEP	

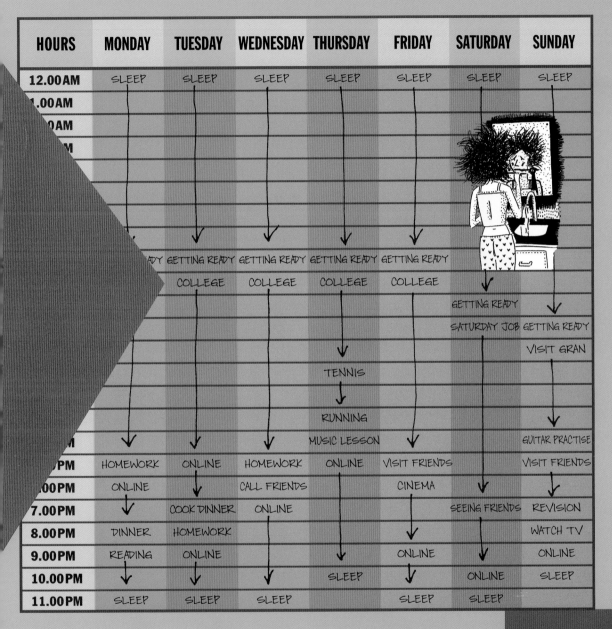

THERE ARE TWENTY-FOUR HOURS TO PLAY WITH

4. WHEN SHOULD I WORK?

There is absolutely no set answer to this question. You know yourself, so just ask yourself, "When do I work best?"

Some people prefer working late at night and others prefer early mornings. It can change as well. You may have been an early morning person and are now a late night person (or vice versa). Once you've discovered when your brain is feeling most active, that's the time to schedule in any work. Just make sure you're not working late at night because you've been procrastinating all day (or even all week) and tomorrow is the deadline.

EACH TO HIS OWN

5. WHERE CAN I WORK?

Everyone has a place which is special, and where they can go to do things.

It may be that you find it easier to think at the library than in your bedroom. You might love hanging out at your local park or writing in a nearby coffee shop.

You're in charge

The only person who can organize you is you. It's important for you to feel that you're in charge of your days rather than your days running away with you. Find environments you like, so that you can be organized and in control. If your home isn't right, find somewhere else.

PETER'S STORY

Peter really wanted to paint. He hadn't painted since he was quite young at school but he'd enjoyed it then and felt he wanted to do more now. His mum was quite strict about mess and didn't like Peter using paints at home. No matter how much he told her he would clear up properly, she dismissed his idea. Peter decided to investigate all the local classes around him and in the end he found a local evening class where he could not only paint, but do silk-screen printing, pottery and all sorts of creative things. He had made a nest for himself outside his own home.

FIND YOUR OWN PLACES

"One of the advantages of being disorderly is that one is constantly making exciting discoveries."
A. A. Milne

The word "discovery" is a great way of thinking about creativity, because once you stop being curious, you stop being creative. It is important to ask questions and be nosy and not box yourself in with "don't likes", beliefs and assumptions. This chapter will help you to open up your thinking and realize the creative person you are.

2. WHAT IF I DON'T FEEL

One of the simplest and most creative pursuits is brainstorming. You probably do it without thinking when you're deciding with friends what you want to do for the evening.

Everybody shouts out ideas of what you could do. The first idea might be quite ordinary: *go to the cinema, eat out, hang out at your place, go clubbing,* but they might end up becoming more and more creative: *go on a road trip, bake a cake at my place, go camping* and so on.

Freeing your mind

Brainstorming is fun because it frees your brain, allowing it to come up with anything and everything. It's only when you start relaxing that the creative magic happens.

You can brainstorm with friends or on your own. Brainstorming can be used at any time – whether you want to think of a present to buy for someone or if you have an art project to do.

Push it to the next level

Brainstorm with a "random seed". Imagine you and your friends were brainstorming where to go on holiday. If you throw in a random seed, for example a frying pan, you can suddenly relax and get more creative. Start brainstorming around the frying pan – frying pans are hot (let's go somewhere hot), frying pans are used for cooking (let's go on a cooking holiday), frying pans are used to cook eggs (let's stay on a farm), frying pans are made of metal (let's visit a tin mine in Cornwall) and on it goes until you come up with a load of ideas. You can use any nouns as random seeds: trumpet, car, chair, magic, lamp and so on.

BOUNCE IDEAS AROUND

CREATIVE?

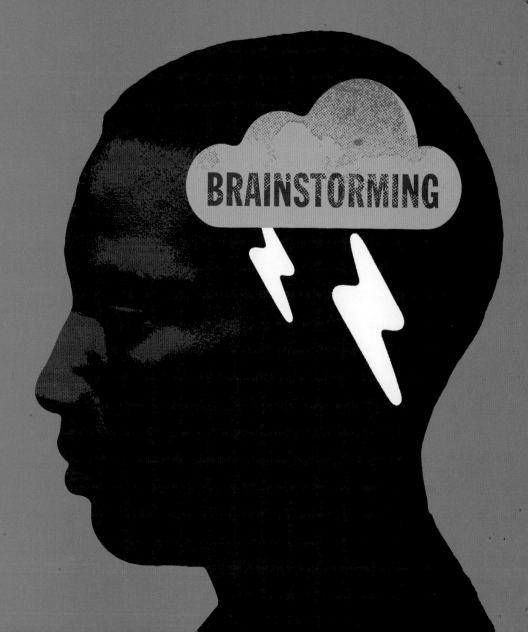

BRAINSTORMING

3. HOW CAN I SOLVE PROBLEMS CREATIVELY?

Have you ever played around with metaphors like, "he raced into the room like a rocket" or "the light shone as brightly as the sun"?

Metaphors are surprisingly useful in helping solve problems. They push you out of your usual way of thinking and instantly get you thinking more creatively.

Using metaphors

The way you use metaphors to solve your problem is to think of two metaphors – a "before" (Metaphor 1) and an "after" (Metaphor 2).

Starting with Metaphor 1, make a drawing (it doesn't have to be a masterpiece, stickmen are fine) of the way you feel now. If you're not seeing your grandmother enough, Metaphor 1 might be a globe with both of you on different sides of it.

Then draw Metaphor 2 – the way you'd like to feel. Again, that could be you and Granny hugging.

Finally think about how you could get from Metaphor 1 to Metaphor 2.

You'll find that using a visual detaches you from your problem. You feel that it isn't your problem any more, which helps you step back and come to conclusions more easily.

JAKE'S STORY

Jake was particularly nervous about a presentation he had to give to his study group. His Metaphor 1 was of himself inside a cage full of lions. Each of them had their mouth open as if they were go ing to eat him. His Metaphor 2 showed him with all the same lions, only this time they were in a circus tent and he was the ringmaster with the whip and the lions were obediently walking around the ring. This was the situation Jake wanted, but how could he get from Metaphor 1 to Metaphor 2?

Jake could see that as a ringmaster he looked pretty confident. Thinking about what usually gave him confidence, Jake realized that he had to be fully prepared, so there wouldn't be any surprises. He started reading up on everything he'd need to know for the presentation. Jake also knew that listening to music always made him feel good, so he decided he'd listen to his most upbeat tracks just before the presentation started. Finally Jake wondered how he could recreate the ringmaster's whip. He thought he could take a pencil into the presentation with him which he could hold in his hand (or even just keep in his pocket) as he spoke, to give him that extra feeling of being in charge.

USE
PICTURES
TO FIND
ANSWERS

4. HOW CAN I THINK DIFFERENTLY?

Metaphors will help you think differently, as will mixing with different groups of people and experiencing different things. Asking yourself different questions will free your thinking too.

5. DOES I

> **There is nothing new except what has been forgotten.**
> Marie Antoinette

Too often we equate creativity with originality, but the two things are not the same.

When we're being creative it is easy to put someone down for not coming up with an idea that is totally new. There are few truly original thoughts left, few truly original ideas and few totally original products. Yet the putting together of thoughts and/or actions in different ways is always original and creative, because it's you that's doing it. Don't worry about whether you are being original, just do things and learn things and you'll find you're being highly creative.

**DO THINGS
YOUR
OWN WAY**

MATTER IF I'M NOT ORIGINAL?

JIM'S STORY

One day when Jim was a boy he saw a futuristic action figure that he really liked and he bought it. Eleven years later he did a degree course in robotics, which included making a robot. The robot he made was modelled on the futuristic action figure. It did everything his childhood toy had done, only this time it worked electronically rather than manually. Jim had doubts that his work was creative but his friends assured him that it was and that he should be proud of himself. He had taken an old idea and made it his own by doing it his own way.

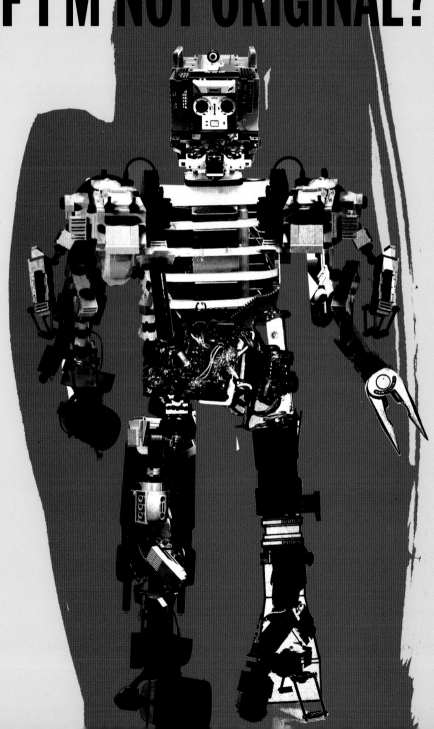

6. HOW CAN I FEEL MORE

You can become creative
at any time and in any place.

Creativity comes when you aren't thinking about
being creative. Don't put pressure on yourself.

Five ways to help you feel creative

1. Change: Creativity
comes when you are doing
something slightly out of the
ordinary such as having a
picnic or moving furniture.

3. Inspiration: Creativity can
come from being inspired. You
might be inspired by other people,
by going to an art gallery or by
listening to music.

2. Stress: Creativity can come in
semi-stressful situations, such as
wanting to ask someone out or being
stuck outside your home with no
keys and no way of getting in. You are
forced to think differently.

4. Relaxation: Creativity
can hit you when you're
relaxing – having a bath
or going for a walk.

CREATIVE?

Am I already creative?

Whether you're thinking a different thought from normal, learning something new or creating something from scratch, you're being creative.

Get creative

Stop thinking about whether you're creative or not. Instead do something out of your routine and relax. See what happens.

5. Boredom: Creativity often comes when you get so bored you start to do something yourself.

YOU ARE CREATIVE ALREADY

7. HOW DO I KICK-START

Often creativity is stopped by the "teacher" in your mind being too judgemental.

A little voice inside your head says, "You're no good at art" or "Stop being so silly" and yet silliness can be just what's needed to start being creative. If you can, turn off that "teacher" until you want to evaluate what you've created.

There is no "wrong"

What's important to remember when you kick-start your creativity is that there is no such thing as a mistake. Each "mistake" can become part of the solution, especially when brainstorming.

MY CREATIVITY?

Be silly

Ideas flow best when you're relaxed – possibly
even being a little silly. If you put pressure on
yourself to be creative you'll freeze up and
won't be able to do anything at all. Start by
relaxing and allowing your brain to free-flow.
Creativity is as much about attitude as it is
about ability. Believe you are creative, trust
you are creative and, if no solution comes to
you, just stop looking and do something else.

OFTEN THE BEST IDEAS COME TO
YOU WHEN YOU LEAST EXPECT THEM.

**RELAX
AND
TRUST**

"Life is a process of becoming, a combination of states we have to go through. Where people fail is that they wish to elect a state and remain in it. This is a kind of death."
Anaïs Nin

You may never think about change as it's something that happens so much it is impossible to imagine life without it.

There are some changes that really do change your life – like moving house or school or job or when someone you love dies. There are other smaller changes that happen too that may not be as dramatic but can still affect you – such as gaining a friend or losing one. And there are those changes – getting older, gaining weight and your hair growing – that happen so slowly that you hardly notice them.

For finding out who you want to be, the most important type of changes are the changes you make deliberately. In order to change, you will undoubtedly have to push yourself in some way or another and that can feel like an uncomfortable process.

Happiness
Imagine your life as an enormous bicycle wheel you're sitting on. When you're at the top of the wheel things look all rosy (let's call that place **happiness**).

1. WHY DO I DISLIKE CHANGE?

This metaphor is taken from a medieval drawing showing Fortune as a woman holding a large wheel. It illustrates how people are all tossed around by external change and that suffering is an inevitable part of change.

Hope
The wheel moves round again and you're at 9 o'clock, knowing that you're about to reach the top (9 o'clock is **hope**). One more movement, and you are at the top and the circle goes round again.

Loss
As the wheel goes round you slip down to the 3 o'clock position, and suddenly life is looking a little bit more dodgy (that place is called **loss**).

Suffering
The wheel moves round again and you're right at the bottom, almost underneath the wheel at 6 o'clock, and things are looking bad (we call that place, **suffering**).

SADNESS IS AS VALUABLE AS HAPPINESS

Change involves suffering

We can never omit the suffering part of the wheel's journey, but the journey round the wheel can take different amounts of time. For example, if someone you love dies, you may find yourself in suffering for a long time. The wheel may appear to swing to hope and possibly even happiness, but it may feel as if it keeps returning to suffering all the time. However, not all journeys will take a long time.

ESTHER'S STORY

Esther had decided to start revising. It was almost exam time and today was the day. She woke up feeling happy – she had made a decision. The morning started well; she tidied her desk and got out her first subject ready to go. Then her mother called and asked if she could babysit her little sister, Hannah, for a few hours. Esther went straight into loss as she could see her revision not happening and then, almost instantly, dived into suffering as Hannah came into her room and started making a mess. Then Esther had a brainwave. She remembered the girl who lived next door. Esther felt hopeful. When she took Hannah round to find out if the neighbour was free to play, they invited Hannah to stay there. Esther felt happy. She was back on track again. The wheel had gone round in a short time.

NICK'S STORY

This wheel took a longer time to go round: Nick had decided to stop smoking. He felt really happy because he'd made a decision about giving up and was sticking to it. Breakfast went well but by mid-morning Nick was in loss and desperate for a cigarette. The reality of giving up had hit him. By the end of the day, even though this was a change he wanted to make, Nick was tense, stressed and had a raging headache. He was definitely in suffering. It took a couple of weeks for Nick to get out of suffering and into hope, but it was worth it. He suddenly realized that he was going to be OK without smoking – and that was happiness.

Use suffering

We often dread or fear change because of the suffering it can cause. But both Esther and Nick came out of their experiences wiser and more fulfilled. Suffering is not a place to be avoided. It's a place to be embraced – just like happiness. Both bring new experiences and both bring growth and understanding. Rather than trying to avoid suffering, use it.

How do you cope with change?

How you choose to react when change happens is up to you. If your friend can't come over, do you go into loss or find something else to do? If your holiday is cancelled, do you go into suffering or do you choose a different holiday? You decide on the impact you want change to have.

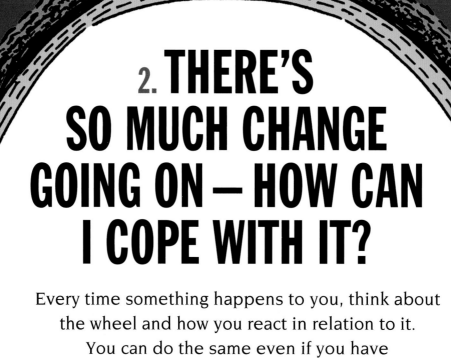

2. THERE'S SO MUCH CHANGE GOING ON – HOW CAN I COPE WITH IT?

Every time something happens to you, think about the wheel and how you react in relation to it. You can do the same even if you have caused or want to cause your own change. Here are three ways of coping with change.

1. See your life as a whole

One way of lessening the force of change is to see your life as a whole and to notice how all aspects of your life are changing all the time, even if sometimes you're just focusing on one or two. Review your life. See where on the wheel you are in all the other parts of your life. Balance the sadness you are feeling in some areas with the happiness you may be feeling in others.

2. Get closer to the centre of the wheel

The second way of feeling less impacted by change is by thinking how you could get closer to the centre of the wheel where the movement is less severe. There will always be some things that calm you down and help you cope with the changes. You might relax more hanging out with friends, listening to music, meditating, going for a long walk or running. Things that help you relax will also help you get to the centre of the wheel, so find out what works for you.

3. Find a different perspective

The third way of feeling better about change is to see if you can find the silver lining within the cloud. Remember back to other times when things have gone badly and reflect on the good things that came out of those difficult periods. Trust that everything will turn out all right in the end.

LOOK AT LIFE IN A FEW DIFFERENT WAYS

3. AM I READY FOR CHANGE?

You might dread change, but usually indecision is worse.

Sitting on the fence, when you keep on asking yourself, "Do I want to do that?", "Am I ready to do that?", "Is this the right time to do that?" is difficult. Once you go for it, change usually makes you feel better. Or if you deliberately decide not to change, that will make you feel better, too.

Different perspectives

Perspectives can be very helpful in decision-making. Think of being in the same situation you are in now, only in the future. In this perspective you imagine doing absolutely nothing about the situation you are in now for three years and seeing what happens.

For example, if you're thinking about getting fitter, but can't really be bothered, imagine yourself three years from now, still not having exercised at all and work out how you'd look, how you'd feel, what you'd think about yourself. Now do you feel motivated? Are you ready for change?

IMAGINE A FUTURE WITHOUT CHANGE

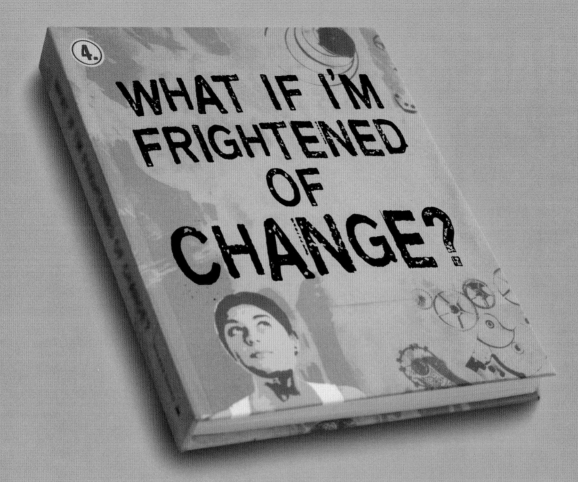

4. WHAT IF I'M FRIGHTENED OF CHANGE?

Part of what stops you changing anything is a feeling that everything will happen all at once.

But change often happens in tiny little invisible steps that you hardly notice. There's no need to worry about anything happening instantly – it will usually be lots of changes and hard work that will make things happen, not the wave of a fairy wand.

Get your mind used to change

Fool your mind into thinking you've already changed, so when you do, you're mentally prepared for it. Let's say you want to write a novel or play football for your local team. If in your mind you begin to imagine that you've already written that novel or that you already play football for your local team, you'll probably start to feel differently about yourself. These different feelings may make you start focusing more on your writing or practising football more. You'll start acting the part, and those first few steps will happen automatically.

5. CAN I CHANGE ANYONE ELSE?

Has your mum ever said she wished she could get you to work harder?

Did it work? Did her saying it make you work harder? Probably not. At best she might have made you feel guilty for a few minutes during which time you got out some books, but it didn't change you.

You change if you want to

People change because they want to change or, sometimes, simply because they're growing up. Intrinsically they stay the same. There are ways in which they can change – but only if they want to.

What's wrong with them?

If you want someone to change, start by thinking, "Why?" Why do you want them to change? Maybe it's more about what they're mirroring in you that's annoying. As you can't change anyone else – maybe you might want to change yourself.

ELLIE'S STORY

Ellie was fed up with her boyfriend, John, because he always stayed in. Whenever they were invited to parties, Ellie would go, but John would make some sort of excuse and stay at home. Ellie started getting angry with John. "You're so anti-social. Why can't you come to parties and talk to people like everyone else? You're a hermit and I'd like you to change." John and Ellie decided to have a serious talk about this, as his behaviour was clearly upsetting Ellie. What came out of their discussion was that Ellie, too, wanted to stay at home, but felt that if neither of them went out they'd get a reputation for being anti-social. She disliked him being so selfish because it meant **she** couldn't be selfish. John and Ellie decided to take it in turns to go to parties so that Ellie could stay in sometimes, too.

Sometimes, rather than trying to change someone, it's good to talk about it and see whether you can't compromise. It's a way of both of you changing – because you want to.

YOU CAN
REALLY ONLY
CHANGE
YOURSELF

6. DO I NEED TO CHANGE!?

Only you know if you want to change.

But just the fact that you are thinking you might want to change something about yourself or your life, means that you probably do.

Change leads to security

It's usually easier to get on and do things than be constantly fearful. Ironically, you can become more secure if you take chances on things that you're worrying about.

You can say to yourself, "I was dreading doing that and I did it – and, what's more, it was quite easy, so now I can do the next thing I'm dreading." Change can give you confidence. Take it one step at a time.

Reflect

Look back over all the times you've changed something about yourself or your life and think about how it felt. Remember how worried you were before those changes and think about how they worked out. Use your past experiences to give you confidence for the future.

Jump!

Imagine a stone hitting the water. You're that stone. Throw yourself in and get yourself wet. Once you've taken the plunge, your courage will grow – just like those ripples do.

CONTROLLED CHANGE CREATES CONFIDENCE

Friends like you as you are. Why on earth would they want you to change? In their minds if you changed you might leave them and go off with other people.

It's in their interest to keep you just as you are. But is it in your interest? When you change you don't have to change everything. Just how much you change is up to you.

GEMMA'S STORY

There was no doubt about it, Gemma was overweight. She was one of those very cheerful girls who everyone was friends with, but she struggled with her figure. She was too young to be quite so large and couldn't buy clothes in the same shops as her friends because she was just too big to find anything on their racks. Gemma wanted to lose weight but her friends said, "Gemma, we love you as you are – you don't have to lose any weight. Anyway, you may not be 'you' once you lose weight." Gemma did not want to upset her friends – plus it was easier not to diet – so she stayed fat and "happy".

One day Gemma decided she'd had enough. From now on she was going to put herself first and go on a diet. "If my friends are so fickle as to care about how I look, I don't want them as friends," she said to herself.

Over the following months, Gemma lost quite a bit of weight. She felt healthier, she looked great and she could now shop in the same stores as her friends and, surprise, surprise, she was just as cheerful as she had always been – only now she wasn't using her humour to distract others from her weight, but just because she enjoyed laughing.

BE WHO YOU WANT TO BE

> **"Work, love and play are the great balance wheels of man's being."**
>
> Orison Swett Marden

In our society we know we thrive on a balanced diet, but why link balance solely to meals? Think about balance in terms of work, love, sleep and play – and the rest of your life.

Balance is essential to your being. Are you balancing laughter with tears, moving with staying still, friends with alone-time? You'll notice the balance you want in your life right now is totally different from the balance your parents want or your younger siblings might want. You'll also find you'll change the balance you want at various periods of your life. What's vital is to find the balance you want now.

One of the things that causes you to lose balance is stress.

There are so many little things (let alone big things) to worry about and these worries can stop you relaxing.

Worrying creates a vicious circle

The annoying thing is that the more you stress, the more you stress. It's a vicious circle and one which will stop you feeling calm and in control, and stop you functioning properly.

Sort out your worries

It's a good idea to divide up your worries so you can eliminate those you can't do anything about. Go round your Balance Chart (p30), using it to remind you of everything that's going on in your life, and write down everything you're worried about. Then divide all of your worries into three groups.

BALANCED?

1. Worries that will get better anyway given time – even if you do nothing at all, for example:
- Your bad haircut will grow out.
- You will be able to leave your parents' home at some stage.
- Your younger brother will grow up and stop annoying you in front of your friends.

2. Worries you can't do anything about, for example:
- It may rain tomorrow even though you're working outside.
- Your train might be delayed in the morning.
- You might get dumped.
- Your dad's girlfriend might move in.

3. Worries with a practical solution that you can do something about, for example:
- The cinema may be full up when you get there – but you can book tickets in advance.
- You're working all day tomorrow and may get hungry – but you could take a packed lunch with you.
- You haven't written your essay outline yet – but you could get out of bed and do it now.

Worrying stops you sleeping

If you're someone who stays awake worrying, work out which worries you can do something about and which you can't. Then, for all those you can do something about, work out the practical solutions before you go to sleep. You'll find you'll sleep better having thrown half your problems away and solved the others.

KNOW WHICH PROBLEMS YOU CAN SOLVE – AND WHICH YOU CAN'T

2. HOW CAN I MAKE MYSELF HAPPIER?

You can make yourself sad by dwelling on things going on in your life that you don't like.

Making yourself happy is just the same. You can dwell on the good things in your life – the things you like – and that way, make yourself feel happier and grateful for having them.

Three tips for feeling happier

1. Find things that absorb you

You probably know what it feels like when you are so involved that you forget everything around you, including what time it is. Absorption comes from being creative – fully involved in an activity that means something to you. You're completely focused on the now and feel in flow. It could be painting, playing the violin, swimming or working – anything that you find completely engrossing.

Although these times don't happen often, it's been shown that doing more of what leads you to absorption can definitely make you happier. Notice every time it happens and keep a list so you can build these things into your life.

2. Think about others as well as yourself (or vice versa)

This is where the balance comes in. You probably find that you veer in one direction, finding either thinking about yourself or about others easier, but if you can find a perfect balance, that will bring you happiness.

Listen out for who you're talking about and who you're thinking about and who you're doing things for. Is it you or someone else?

PATTI'S STORY

Patti was incredibly good at looking after herself. Her nails were always beautifully painted, her hair shone, she got enough sleep and she always wore great clothes. In so many ways Patti's life was perfect and yet she didn't feel happy. One day her boyfriend fell off his bike and hurt his leg badly so he couldn't walk. Patti's first thought was that they were going to miss the party that night, she felt angry with him and frustrated, especially as she'd just bought a new dress to wear. When Patti arrived at his house and saw him sitting there, looking a little battered and bruised, something inside her changed. Patti made him a cup of tea and changed his bandages. For the first time ever, she fussed over him and forgot about herself. That evening was a turning point for Patti. She realized how happy she felt looking after someone else and decided to visit her granny more often.

3. Feel in control

One way of feeling in control is to strike a balance between focusing on the past, the future and the present. Living in the now provides a very immediate form of happiness and helps you feel in control.

You may notice that when you spend too much time looking backwards you can feel regret or guilt or sadness. This is fine, but again, keep a balance. Setting goals and being focused on the future, and what you want from it, can be a good antidote to living in the past and will make you feel more in control and happier.

What would make you happy?

Go round your Balance Chart (p30) and imagine how it would feel if you scored a ten in each area. What would it take for you to be happy in each area?

THINK WHAT MAKES YOU HAPPY

I'M DOING THE RIGHT THINGS?

There are no standard right things to do, what's important is whether you're doing the right things for you.

The Balance Chart (p30) is something you can revisit week after week. Just keep checking in and seeing if you feel your life is going the way you want it to go. You're not aiming for your scores on the Balance Chart to be a perfect circle (though that may happen if you're doing what you want to do), you're aiming for it to reflect what you want from your life. The Balance Chart is a snapshot of what's going on in your life. It will point out that you're not looking after yourself or aren't feeling happy or are arguing with your family and then it's up to you to decide if you're happy with the status quo or want to do something about it.

Escaping from habits

People often over-indulge in one area. You might get addicted to exercise or eating or smoking or spending money or the Internet or lying in bed. It's not necessarily a real addiction (though if it's smoking or drugs it may be), but these habits take up a lot of time and stop your life feeling balanced.

Breaking the pattern

Sometimes the reason you keep your habits is because you don't know what to replace them with. What, for example, would you be doing if you weren't social networking online? If you want to break the pattern you're in, you may have to rearrange your life completely. Wouldn't it be great if you could replace your habit with something from an area you're doing less in? That's what balance is all about.

Is it really me?

Just because you've got a habit doesn't mean you are your habit. It's separate from you and as such can be got rid of. It's up to you to decide if this habit is what you want and, if it isn't, to stop it. Start noticing when you're over-indulging. Is it always at the same time of day? Is it always with the same friends? Is it always when you're on your own? When you're bored? When you're at home? When you've had a fight? What is that habit helping you avoid?

Notice what you're doing

Keep a list or a diary of when you over-indulge. Then ask yourself what you're doing it instead of, and choose to do something else.

YOU ARE NOT YOUR HABIT

4. DO I HAVE TO DO THE THINGS I DON'T LIKE DOING?

The short answer may well be "Yes".

There are probably many things you don't like doing that you still have to do (even if only occasionally) because otherwise you will upset other people, or let yourself down. There are also things that you have chosen to do at some stage in your life that you may want to drop now and that's absolutely fine, so long as you're not hurting anyone. You're aiming for the balance that you want, a balance that fits into your life and those who are part of it.

Do you know what you like doing?

Often we don't know what we want from life, but we do know what we don't want. It's like standing in front of a counter full of different kinds of sweets and being asked to choose what sweets you want. You may know immediately or you may find it easier to eliminate all those you don't want, until you're left with the one you do. Getting rid of the things you don't want in your life helps you focus on the ones you do. It gives you extra time and energy to get on with the things you do like doing.

In order to find the balance you want, you have to get to know yourself really well. It's a matter of trusting your intuition and understanding if your life is going the way you want it to or if you're being influenced by others and taken off in a direction that isn't you.

TIM'S STORY

Tim and Freddy had been tennis partners from the age of five. As a team they were unbeatable and were thrilled because they'd got into Junior Wimbledon for the next summer. But somewhere deep down their relationship was no longer working. Tim noticed that they rarely did high-fives in between points any more and that if he, Tim, went up to Freddy to say, "Well done!", Freddy would sort of dismiss Tim and make him feel small. One day their coach said to Tim, "What's wrong?" Tim didn't really know what was wrong. The coach went on, "If there was something you need never do again, what would it be?" The coach half expected Tim to say, "I don't want to practise as hard as I do", but Tim looked him right in the eyes and, as if from nowhere, suddenly knew what he had to say, "I don't want to play tennis with Freddy again". Tim found a new partner and is still playing tennis – and winning – but not with Freddy.

YOU KNOW WHAT YOU DON'T WANT

**Success is not the key to happiness.
Happiness is the key to success.
If you love what you are doing,
you will be successful.**
Albert Schweitzer

Success means different things
to different people.

SUCCESS

1. HOW CAN I BE HAPPY?

All roads lead to happiness

Happiness is almost the only thing we want just for itself. If you think about your Balance Chart, the areas where you want to score ten are the ones you think will make you happier. If you want to score ten in Creativity, it's because you feel that being more creative will make you happier. Although happiness is often one of our main goals, it's almost impossible to aim for. You reach it by making yourself happy in specific areas of your life.

Seven keys to happiness

There are a few things you can do to start making yourself happier. Let's call them the "keys" to happiness. They have been identified from the characteristics that happy people have in common. Why not have a go at one-a-day for a week. Be aware of how you feel when you're trying each one.

The answer to that question depends on your perspective.

If you see life through a "my glass is half-empty" (negative) lens, you'll be more cautious and find it difficult to notice the good things in life. But if you see things through a "my glass is half-full" (positive) lens, you'll find it easier to notice how happy you are.

1. Happy people often feel connected

The more you feel a part of something, the happier you'll be. For example, you can feel connected when you're stroking a cat or examining a beautiful flower, being with people or listening to music.

2. Happy people think about others as well as themselves

This one is a loop. The happier you are, the more you'll want to think about others and reach out to them and the more you think about them and reach out to them, the happier you'll become. Could you visit your grand-parents more? Could you do some voluntary work? Remember to keep some "me-time" too.

3. Happy people feel in control of their lives

If you focus on what you want out of your life, and set goals, you'll feel in control. If you wallow in the past and pick over what went wrong, you're going to become less confident and less in control. Focus on the present – or even the future – rather than the past, and you'll start feeling more in control.

4. Happy people get absorbed in what they're doing

Being in the present can make you happy. Do you know those moments when you're doing something that you're so engrossed in that you lose track of everything? It's as if time stands still. Find out the things that absorb you. It might be painting, playing the guitar or walking through autumn leaves. When you have these moments, write them down as they are one of the keys to happiness for you.

5. Happy people have high self-esteem

It's another loop. Those of us who like ourselves and feel good about ourselves tend to feel good about life too. And, once you feel good about life, you'll start feeling good about yourself.

6. The lives of happy people have a meaning or purpose

Happy people usually have something meaningful in their lives which gives them a reason for living – a purpose. It could be going travelling or wanting to be a doctor. Start small and work out what outcome you want from each day.

7. Happy people take risks

As you've seen before, happiness comes from taking risks, stepping out of your comfort zone, challenging yourself and getting out of a rut (p60). Often knowing your purpose will give you the confidence to try new things.

DISCOVER YOUR KEYS TO HAPPINESS

2. HOW CAN I BE SUCCESSFUL NOW?

Often when we feel successful, it's because we've finished what we started. So, in order to feel successful, whatever it is you're doing has to have an end.

Having an idea and not completing it won't make you happy, nor will giving up and stopping half-way through what you're doing.

Not appreciating success

If, even after finishing something, you don't feel successful, it may be because what you set out to do was too "easy", so you don't appreciate having done it. Or maybe you didn't define what you wanted to achieve.

Non-specific goals

Often our goals are too open. Neither "I want to be happy" nor "I want to be rich" will make you feel successful, as you haven't defined exactly what "happy" or "rich" are, so you will never be able to achieve them. In order to be successful, be specific when goal-setting and notice that you're achieving what you set out to do.

Feel successful now

Go ahead and finish something now – yes, right now. Think of all the things you need (or want) to do and make a list of them. There may be an essay to write, some reading to do, a card to make and so on. Make a list of all of them and finish just one thing so you can tick it off your list.

Keep a record of your successes – each and every one of them. Put them in a special "Record of Achievements" file – they're all worth celebrating.

DEFINE YOUR GOAL AND ACHIEVE IT

3. WHAT IF I GET THINGS WRONG?

"Wrong" is an essential stage on the way to success. Thomas Edison, inventor of the light bulb, had many "wrong" attempts in his inventions but said that his "failures" were needed in order for him to succeed.

Here are two of his famous sayings:
"Our greatest weakness lies in giving up. The most certain way to succeed is always to try just one more time."
"I have not failed. I've just found 10,000 ways that won't work."

Failure equals learning

Failure isn't failing at what you attempt to do, (although it can feel like it at the time), failing is not attempting at all – staying as you are. Each time you "fail" you learn a lesson which will put you in a stronger, better position to succeed the next time.

Problems equal success

See problems as a time of growth and development. Rather than jump to an "I'm not good enough" conclusion, allow what you learn from the "failure" to help you attempt whatever it is you want to achieve again – only differently – this time with a plan B.

FAILURE LEADS TO SUCCESS

4. HOW CAN I DO THINGS BETTER?

At school you have teachers who keep you on track, make you arrive on time and hand in your homework.

When you're not at school, you're really only accountable to yourself. Make sure you're doing what you want to do.

Being down on yourself

Most of the time you probably feel OK about the way you're living your life, but there may be days when you feel down on yourself and as if you're not doing anything "well". You may be over-eating, or haven't been to the gym in months or kept up with your friends or maybe you're wasting time sitting in front of the TV.

Keep things in perspective

When you start feeling like this, take a good look at your life as a whole. Maybe you're not stepping up all the time at work or college, but possibly you've got a fantastic relationship with your partner. It's always your decision as to where in your life you put your energy.

Break down your life by making a list of what you could be doing better (where you're letting yourself down) and a list of what you're doing well. See your behaviour as a whole. We often do things we find easy or that give us the results that we want. If you look at the list you just wrote, think about what makes it easy for you to be proactive in the areas you're doing well in and what makes you let yourself down in others.

When you know what makes it easy for you to be accountable, you can work out ways of becoming accountable in other areas. For example, you may be really good at hockey. When you ask yourself "why" you like hockey, you realise it's because hockey is a team game and it provides you with a rush of adrenaline. It's these things that keep you practising.

In your list of things you are doing well in, ask yourself why you find it easy to do well in each of these areas. Then work out how those "whys" could be used in the list of what you could be doing better.

Imagine you phone up your friends every day and never forget their birthdays, but eat junk food, rather than salads and fresh fruit. What is it that makes calling your friends so easy? Maybe by calling your friends you get a feeling of belonging and being popular. Think how eating healthy food can give you these feelings of belonging and being popular. Perhaps you could eat in company, rather than on the run? Or you could find a group of friends who want to change their eating habits, too. Use the "whys" to help you make those changes.

MAKE THINGS WORK FOR YOU

5. DO I HAVE TO BE RICH TO BE SUCCESSFUL?

One of the biggest successes is when you can wholeheartedly enjoy being yourself. That often doesn't cost any money.

Instead it involves really knowing yourself – who you are and what you enjoy doing – so that if you have a blank day in your diary to spend on your own, you'll look forward to it.

Be your own best friend

People usually think that feeling successful involves rewarding themselves, say with a shopping trip, but if you wanted to show your best friend you cared for them, would you go out and buy them something? You might give them a present, but you might simply pay them a compliment or do something nice for them, or simply spend time with them. Do the same for yourself.

Think positively about yourself

Notice when you're doing something well and praise yourself. In your mind, see yourself as the small child you once were – you're not really that different now – and take good care of that child. For this type of success there's no need to spend any money at all.

SUCCESS IS BEING YOUR OWN BEST FRIEND

As well as being a good friend to yourself, be the best friend that you can be to others. Start by deciding what you think a good friend would be like, and then you'll know what to aim for.

What makes a good friend?

Go through the list below thinking about the qualities a good friend might have and tick the ones that are important to you.

Here are some ideas to get you started. Would they ...

- have a great sense of humour?
- like the same things you do?
- do the same things you do?
- believe in the same things you do?
- be honest with you?
- be reliable?
- confident in you?
- keep your confidences?
- teach you new things?
- be able to learn from you?
- listen to you?
- have an interesting way of thinking?
- be knowledgeable in a different field to you?
- be very different to you?
- be very similar to you?
- look up to you?
- enjoy you looking up to them?
- smile a lot?
- give compliments freely and genuinely?
- be encouraging?
- be interested in you – even curious?
- be exciting?

Are you a good friend?

Once you've discovered what you think a good friend is, go through the list again, this time ticking the characteristics that would describe you – do the ticks fall in the same places? We all have the ability to have all of these qualities. Are there any characteristics that you could improve on?

WHAT DO YOU WANT FROM A FRIEND?

7. HOW CAN I HAVE A GREAT LONG-TERM RELATIONSHIP?

Now you've found self-love and discovered who you are on your own, there is no reason why you can't be successful in a long-term relationship. Choose someone to be with that you respect and remain as independent and respectful of each other as you can.

Think long-term

Think about all the long-term relationships you have with your family and friends and see what made it easy for you to be in them.

YOU'RE GOOD AT RELATIONSHIPS

This book is a part of Life Clubs, the business that I started in 2004. I want to thank everyone who has worked with me in Life Clubs (you know who you are) as well as those who have been involved with this book – especially Genevieve Hawes, Tiffany McCall and Ruth Needham.

I am so grateful to my children, Michael (21 at time of writing), Frances (19) and Ursula (16) who read the first draft for me and were unbelievably helpful. Thanks also to their younger brother Thomas (10). His is the story of the robot designer.

Robyn Sisman introduced me to the wonderful "commune" that is Walker Books, and I have been bowled over by the professionalism and talents of Denise Johnstone-Burt, Nic Knight and, of course, Paula MacDonald, who made this book look so brilliant.

So many have inspired me throughout the years. I'd like to mention the late Paul Arden, Lucy Sisman, David Eldridge and Dan Price. Thanks also to Julia Robson and Una Goulding who first used Life Clubs with young people and to James Miller and Simon Jones of Living Well, who used Life Clubs with young people for the NHS. And, of course, to Maurits Kalff, our matchmaker.

Thanks and love, as ever, to Nicholas.

First published 2010 by Walker Books Ltd, 87 Vauxhall Walk, London SE11 5HJ

2 4 6 8 10 9 7 5 3 1

Text © 2010 Nina Grunfeld
Illustrations © 2010 Gary Neill, Barnaby Richards and Michelle Thompson

The right of Nina Grunfeld to be identified as author of this work has been asserted by her in accordance with the Copyright, Designs and Patents Act 1988

This book has been typeset in ITC Novarese and Franklin Gothic

Printed in China

British Library Cataloguing in Publication Data:
a catalogue record for this book is available from the British Library

ISBN 978-1-4063-2384-9

www.walker.co.uk
www.lifeclubs.com
www.garyneill.com   www.barnabyrichards.co.uk   www.michelle-thompson.com

To H.M.